Life After Tolle:

A CALL TO COMMUNITY

Kat Van Gunten

Least Bittern Books
Henry County, KY

To all the builders of the New Earth

Inspired by my spiritual sponsor Brian Kratko

Printed in Henry County, KY

Least Bittern Books
147 Marcus St. #4
Pleasureville, KY 40057

© copyright Kat Van Gunten 2016

This is a work of non-fiction, and personal essay. It is mainly a call to community, inspired by the teachings of Eckhart Tolle. A plea to build a New Earth, beginning with ourselves; it is an examination of the way the author incorporates Tolle's teachings in her daily life.

To awaken within the dream is our purpose now. When we are awake within the dream, the ego-created earth-drama comes to an end and a more benign and wondrous dream arises. This is the new earth!

-Eckhart Tolle

Throughout the millennia, the universe has produced extraordinary teachers who point our species gently towards enlightenment, Eckhart Tolle among them.

Enlightenment, he tells us, is not something that has to be attained. It is something that must be recognized within ourselves. It is ongoing, rewarding as it is arduous.

This book is the story of how I, like many people, have used Tolle's teachings to reconnect with Consciousness on a deep level, but <u>still</u> shift in and out of the Now. In this book I address what is most important in being able to *fully live* a life of Presence, and what gets in the way of that.

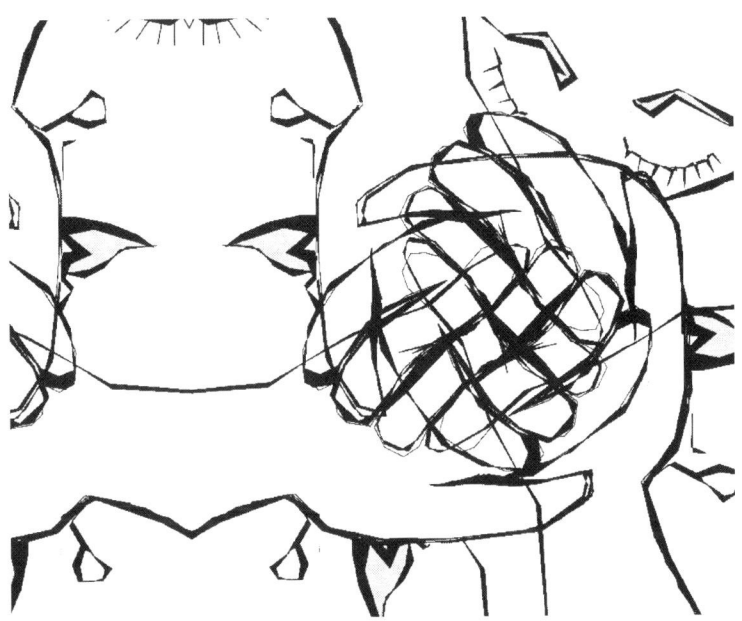

For those of you unfamiliar with Tolle's teachings, before reading on, there are a couple of important concepts that should be understood.

IMPORTANT CONCEPTS

Consciousness: Tolle defines "Consciousness" as spiritual awareness. It is your essence-- who you <u>are</u> underneath your physical and psychological human form. It is your true being, the God in you. Consciousness also represents your inner-state. It is a state of pure **presence**, in which you are free of the thinking **mind**. When you are in touch with Consciousness, you are fully *aware* of what goes on not only around you, but also within you. You are aware of the incessant thoughts your mind churns out, and the emotions that follow. Importantly, you *know* you are *not* those thoughts or emotions. For instance, if one is conscious, and anxiety arises, that person is aware that there is anxiety within; the emotion does not take them over.[2]

Unconsciousness: On the other hand, "unconsciousness," according to Tolle, is a state of non-presence, in which one is totally lost in thought or negative emotions. They are not rooted in themselves. Unconsciousness is the state of the **ego**, or the conditioned **mind**. In other words, being spiritually unconscious means that a person is controlled by the ego and doesn't even know it. They take the sum of their thoughts, emotions and life circumstances to be who they *are*. If one is unconscious, and anxiety arises, that person doesn't *know* they are anxious and the anxiety runs their life. This results in all sorts of avoidance behaviors such as being overly-busy, becoming stressed or creating suffering for themselves and others. It is important, Tolle emphasizes, to be completely conscious in the Now so that you are fully there to face whatever arises.[3]

Although many people are becoming more conscious, most still live in almost complete unconsciousness. They are totally absorbed in the dream of human existence: thoughts, emotions, possessions, career, relationships, success, failure. Awakening happens when you step out of the dream and become aware of who you *are*, underneath your thoughts.[4]

INDIVIDUAL EFFORTS TOWARDS
FULL AWAKENING

CHAPTER ONE
CAN WE FULLY AWAKEN?

For most people, the spiritual-awakening process is a slow one. Sometimes it may feel like forever. "Am I really awakening?" many people wonder.

When you spend an hour in meditation, or take a walk in the park and feel tremendously connected with Life one day, then panic about a relationship breaking down, or money being lost the next, the spiritual journey becomes quite contradictory.

One may even begin to doubt awakening altogether. See, most of us are not the Dali Lama, the Buddha, Jesus Christ, Pema Chodron, Byron Katie or Eckhart Tolle. The majority of people walking the spiritual path have not had a once-and-for-all type of radical enlightenment. While influential men and women provide all we need to know about awakening spiritually, many people continue to walk the Earth in a confused state.

The confusion here comes from the fact that although you realize within yourself the simple, yet deep Truth behind the words of a teacher such as Eckhart Tolle, you often have a difficult time *fully* living such teachings.

Why? Because unlike the author of *The Power of Now,* who stated that he lives completely free from unconscious mind activity, the rest of us who long for total wakefulness possess a mind that simply does not want to leave.

So each day we devote ourselves to practicing present-moment living. We take conscious breaths every now and then, engage in inner body awareness, or just sit in a room in silence, connecting with inner-stillness. Yet despite partaking in these and many other practices Tolle offers, to boost "presence power,"[2] we often get caught up in the busy world around us.

Even after our early-morning meditation, when we drive to work and are running late, our heart-rate increases rapidly, and we go past the speed-limit in a rush to clock-in on time. In other words: we lose ourselves. And most of us get lost every single day, regardless of how deeply devoted we may be to awakening.

In fact, the mind is so strong, and the conditioning so engrained, it seems impossible for us to fully live as someone like Tolle lives! We may have a good week, or even just a couple of days in which we are relatively free from the crazy mind, and are rooted in our true selves. But then we blow up on our partner, and argue for hours because of a comment they made which threatened our ego.

And this is the reality of not only beginners, but also of people who have been eagerly committed to practicing Tolle's present moment teachings for *years*.

*   *   *

In June 2014, I was lucky enough to attend Eckhart Tolle and Kim Eng's 5-day retreat at the world-renown Omega center in Rhineback, NY. When first arriving at the retreat, I was surprised to witness the ego, or unconsciousness, of some of the people around me.

While waiting in a long line the first night, I overheard a group of individuals in front of me indignantly complain about how long it took to check in, and how upset they were that they drove all this way, and would completely miss dinner, and part of Eckhart's opening lecture.

In fact, an hour later, while I was clearly struggling to set up my tent alone, a woman who had just set hers up next to mine rushed past me without offering to help. She mumbled something like, "I don't wanna miss him talk," as she sped by. She was conscious enough to feel funny about not lending a hand. Compelled to acknowledge this verbally, she did not take the minute or two required to assist a fellow-retreater.

Now, it isn't to say I expected every retreat attendee to be fully enlightened. Surely I am not. However, I did not expect to witness such mind-dominance in people at a retreat promoting Consciousness. Further, towards the end of the week, when Tolle's team told the audience that it was alright to take photos of Eckhart and Kim, it was as though Justin Bieber had appeared on stage, and swarms of teenage girls rushed to take pictures of him on their smart phones.

It brought to mind the account of Jesus' frustration, over 2,000 years ago, when he found people selling things in the temple. After driving the people out of the temple, Jesus said:

> It is written, 'My house shall be called a house of prayer,' but you make it a den of robbers!

The people lunging desperately towards the stage to take pictures of Eckhart and Kim in the Main lecture hall of the Omega Center reminded me *even people who are on the awakening journey get overtaken by the ego*. The mind saw in that particular moment a way to capitalize on Eckhart and Kim, as objects to take advantage of. When the people got home, their egos would be enhanced by going up to family members and friends, and showing them that they got so close to the great Eckhart Tolle and Kim Eng.

Their egos, even during that holy time of retreat in that sacred moment, interfered with their own agendas, much like the people in Jesus' time took advantage of the holy temple, by using it as a platform to buy and sell things.

The retreat-goers who eagerly snapped photos at the Omega Center were not in the wrong. I only mention the story as an illustration of the main focus of this book: that millions of people who read Tolle's books, understand his teachings on a deep level, and practice present-moment living can all at once be swept up in an unconscious act.

How is it that something of such great Truth can resonate so deeply in a person, but the person remains stuck shifting back and forth between presence and unconsciousness? In this way, doesn't the unconscious mind steer humanity? And how can we make it so that the average person can live *free of unconsciousness?*

Wouldn't it be nice to actually practice what Tolle teaches each moment? Wouldn't it be wonderful to live in the Now fully, without going off on an ego rampage every few hours? To live without the need to create suffering?

I know it would. This is why I decided to write this book. My friend Brian Kratko provided the inspiration behind it. He and I sometimes call ourselves "average spiritual Joes." We are tired of living a double-life, filled with moments of mind-erasing, awe-inspiring presence in which we feel so alive that nothing else matters, but also arguing with our partners, complaining internally about having to clean the kitchen for the millionth time, or judging our neighbor for wearing "that shirt" again.

*　　*　　*

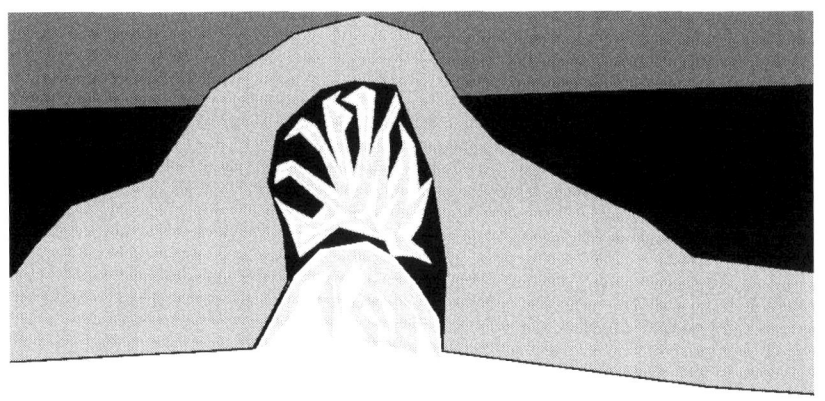

THE DILEMMA OF THE CAVE

While participating in a self-realization class given by Hiram College in the woods of the Upper Peninsula, Michigan, I was introduced to a metaphorical story describing the plight of humanity. The story, which impacts me to this day, is Plato's famous *Allegory of the Cave*.[3]

In the story Plato describes a group of human beings who live inside a cave and perceive the shadows that bounce along the cave walls as reality. These cave-dwellers are absorbed in the shadows, unaware of the world outside the cave.

They have never seen the sky, animals, plants or the light of the sun. There is a small fire inside the cave they constantly sustain to use for warmth. This fire produces shadows on the walls, their only reality. These humans are actually chained inside of this cave. They spend their lives within it, never to know the beauty of life outside.

And yet, one courageous cave-dweller somehow breaks his chains to venture out, into the real world. When the prisoner first leaves the cave, his eyes burn. The light of the sun blinds him.

This is because he has been staring at a dark, blank cave wall covered with shadows his whole life. He is in so much pain, he is tempted to run back into the familiar cave.

Yet, he somehow finds the strength to remain outside the cave's walls. Miraculously, after time, his eyes become accustomed to the natural light. He begins to slowly see the real-life objects surrounding him come into focus. The man is amazed at what he finds: true life all around!

He runs back into the cave and tries to convince the others, who are still consumed in the shadows, to break away and enter reality. Yet, they call him 'crazy.' They refuse to turn from their familiar shadows. They fail to experience life in its fullness.

*

Most people have not yet become awake. They are prisoners in the cave of the human mind, and only experience life through mere shadows- thoughts, conditioning, and emotions.

Plato wrote his *Allegory of the Cave* around 380 BC. Nearly 2,500 years ago, he possessed the clarity to see most humans were overly-immersed in thinking, and not truly alive.

As Tolle often points out, Jesus saw the same thing: people cut off from true life, lost in the shadows of the past and future. Yet, the majority of humans are *still* chained inside their minds! They have not experienced what it is like to know themselves as Consciousness itself, as Tolle teaches. They don't know there is life outside the cave.

All day long cave-dwellers stare at shadows: they watch television, work jobs they may not like so they can make lots of money, drive cars and buy new clothes, drink alcohol, take drugs, overeat, medicate themselves and obsessively *think*.

Why? Because they are afraid of the sunlight. They are afraid of what they would find if they turned away from the shadows, turned off their smart phones and went inside themselves. They would feel pain and discomfort, but don't realize that, as Tolle tells us, beyond the pain awaits true life and abundance, joy and a feeling of wholeness.

So as a society we cling to our chains and gaze at our shadows (habitual thinking and doing) all day long. We refuse to stop even for a moment to step outside the cave. We like the comfort of our conditioning. It's all we know. We don't want to go through the pain of being stripped of our chains and cast into the unknown. This is why we engage in distractions and addictions every day.

We don't want to enter ourselves and feel any pain that may be there. But we must realize that yes, it may burn at first, and make us feel horrible, just as the sun burned the eyes of the cave dweller, but after a while we would be free of that pain. We would see the world around us with new eyes. We would enter into the fullness of life.

Eckhart Tolle represents that brave, first cave-dweller to exit the cave. Through his teachings and lectures he has invited humanity, the rest of the prisoners, to join him and leave the shadows behind. Many have responded to his call. They have left the cave, or their thinking minds. They have discovered within and around themselves the Joy of Being, as Tolle calls it.

In other words, mass amounts of humans, including yourself if you are reading this, have begun the awakening process.

However, whereas Tolle would never return to the cave, most humans on the awakening journey find themselves constantly going back and forth from its comfort. *Even though they have experienced real life outside of the shadows*, they still find themselves at times, bound by chains. These humans are constantly running back and forth, out of the cave and then back into it.

Shifting in and out of the cave is a reality more painful than that of prisoners who have never left the cave. Because once you know and have tasted the bliss of true life outside the mind, or cave, to be thrown back in it is quite difficult.

Millions of humans right now are experiencing this exact reality. They want to live outside of their minds in a state of conscious connectedness with Life, but don't have the strength. And for thousands of years, dating back to the time of the Buddha, Plato, and Jesus, the majority of humans have not had the strength to live free of the mind.

What does this mean? Now is the time we "average spiritual Joe's" who are still bound in some ways to the cave must hold hands, unite and leave it *together*, once and for all. We don't have the individual strength to do it on our own; we must form a community.

A widespread community of awakening humans prepare the way for a New Earth in which the majority of humans live as enlightened beings- rather than just a small minority, as it has been for thousands of years. It is time for cave-dwellers to leave the cave.

CHAPTER TWO
THE MOST IMPORTANT TASK (YOU COULD EVER DO TO BECOME ENLIGHTENED)

We go out of our way to better ourselves. Alcoholics may drive an hour to get to an AA meeting. A devoted Christian may get up early every Sunday for church. A person who overeats, and wants to get in shape may begin a healthy eating plan and exercise regimen. The alcoholic may get sober. The Christian may feel better about him or herself; morally fortified. And the dieter may successfully lose weight.

Anyone reading this can predict what comes next. Even though the alcoholic continues to attend meetings and the Christian goes to church faithfully, those individuals can never be complete or fulfilled unless they realize their true essence, their "Being" as Tolle calls it.[1] They will be a hamster on a wheel, repetitively doing all of these healthy, beneficial things but making no real ground. The overeater who manages to get the weight off will likely gain it back, as is so very common.

Why? Because the person may have run on the treadmill each day and stopped overeating, but did nothing to face the real problem at hand- the deeper issue. Which is what, you may ask? Well, Tolle has said it over and over. If we are not fully present in the Now, it means we are on a constant search for fulfillment in the mind-created future. Deriving completion from the surface layer of life is impossible.[2]

Here's where we come in. Spiritual-seekers do the same thing! We may sit in meditation hour after hour, attend Tuesday night yoga, or save up to attend one of Eckhart Tolle's retreats. We take nature walks regularly, attend lectures, read spiritual books, eat healthfully, get rest we need, watch Super Soul Sunday on the OWN channel, or pay for a monthly membership to EckhartTollenow.com. We form healthy habits, get rid of unhealthy ones, walk the walk and talk the talk. Obviously, we spiritual-seekers want enlightenment.

We crave it more than anything else. We have felt it when reading *The Power of Now* or when looking up at the sky on a silent night and feeling the *space* within as Eckhart poignantly encapsulates.[3] Yet somehow, we cannot seem to hold on to it! At least not for long. But we know how it feels and want to feel it permanently.

However, as I discovered, you can't achieve it by attending an Eckhart Tolle retreat. That alone won't make you undergo a permanent shift from everyday unconsciousness to eternal wakefulness, as I secretly hoped it would. Moreover, traveling to India where the Buddha taught, or to the Holy Land to visit places where Jesus and Mohammed lived doesn't dig deep enough to the root of the problem.

Sobriety, as amazing and awe-inspiring as it is, cannot automatically bring about utter peace, presence and enlightenment. The recovered alcoholic may have solved one addiction, only to then form another, such as overeating or video-streaming. Religious fervor and observation of the Sabbath will not silence the ego for good. And neither will achieving an ideal BMI.

Conversely, even those avid seekers of peace of mind engage in forms of unconsciousness on a daily basis. Compulsive-thinking or egoic wanting, impatience. The spiritual-seeker may listen to Eckhart on tape every day but still constantly judge others, themselves or the present moment as being flawed. Tolle advises us not to be fooled into thinking we don't have any addictions whatsoever, simply because our addictions may be socially acceptable, or hard to detect.

Non-stop thinking, complaining, or always having to be right are forms of egoic addiction, according to Tolle.[4] Addiction of any kind presents a powerful pull from present-moment living. Thus, spiritual-seeking is not unlike being addicted to alcohol: there must be a bigger issue here, which must be dealt with before lasting evolution takes place.

Although we may put in effort on the surface-layer, in order to change ourselves and cease dysfunctional behaviors, we must direct our attention inward.

Eckhart Tolle, in a lecture once said that, "humans rarely face anything."[5]

He is speaking of the deeper dilemma: emotional pain. This is precisely what we go out of our ways to avoid. Mind-made suffering, or pain, is the deeper cause of all problems in our lives. And as anyone reading this knows, emotional pain cannot be completely tackled from the outskirts- the surface-layer of reality.

There has to be an emergence into ourselves in order to dissolve the pain that perpetuates a destructive cycle. If we are unable to go into the pain and face it directly, we will inevitably get sucked into acting out egoic patterns over and over again. Like it or not.

THE SPIRITUAL DOWN FALL

Eckhart Tolle stresses that awakening requires us to focus on the internal, rather than the outer-layer of reality. Yet, even after reading Tolle's words and realizing them on a deep level, many are stuck in the hopeless endeavor of complying with the many commands of our conditioning.

Even when we have all our material needs met, why is it so many of us *still* live in survival mode? We rush from here to there as if the surface-layer of our lives and all its parts are way more important than the inner realm of stillness. Present moment awareness goes out the window all too often.

*

Awakening begins the moment someone realizes they have been sleeping. It happens the moment they notice they are not conscious. Once awakened, a mind can never return to its pre-awakened sate. Once awake, the mind knows the difference between being present or preoccupied. In a sense this makes them accountable for their behaviors in a completely different way. If our doctor tells us our blood-pressure is too high, we know we ought to change our diet, exercise, reduce stress, take a medicine or in other ways see to lowering it.

After first awakening and reading Eckhart Tolle's books I lived life with a child-like wonder, or the "Joy of Being." And this was great. In fact it was beautiful! I felt completely reborn. I saw the world with brand new eyes: awake ones.

I even *felt* like a child again. And Jesus' teaching on becoming like little children points to this. In order to enter the present-moment fully (the kingdom of heaven), one must first lose the heaviness of the ego and awaken (become like children).[6]

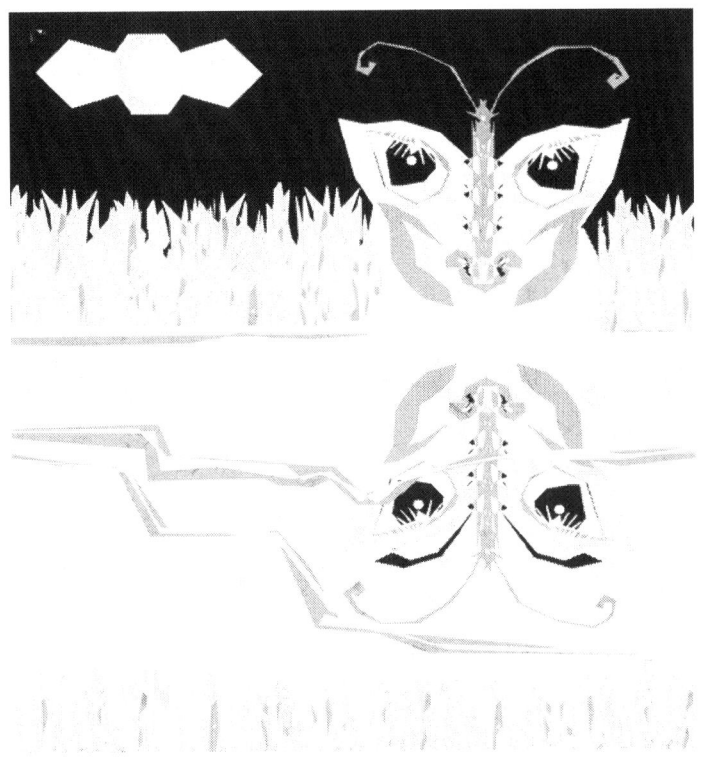

I broke through dense conditioning and reconnected to my true self. Life could not have felt better. I reunited with nature, experienced the true meaning of silence for the first time and discovered with awe the aliveness of my inner body. It was as though I had won the lottery of life. Each day I was rooted in Presence. My life began to change in positive ways.

During this time, I was absolutely gung-ho on anything to do with Eckhart Tolle. I devoted my life to spiritual practice. I even felt slightly proud of this, admittedly, as if I was superior to and separated from lowly humans who had not yet awakened.

Speaking of these other humans, I related to them differently. I was no longer as affected by their unconsciousness.

I saw them for who they were: unawake to their true Being, and thus not conscious of their actions.

My relationships became deeper, more real. I experienced true love. I walked in nature more and felt the aliveness of the birds and the trees that teemed out there. Sometimes, I looked at the leaves on a tree for minutes at a time, just appreciating their beauty.

I practiced meditation, even if it simply meant sitting in silence and noticing the thoughts arise. I listened to Eckhart Tolle on my i-pod, in the car, and on my laptop at home on a daily basis. Similarly, my friend Brian admitted he even listened to Tolle while in the shower.

A vision board filled with quotes from the *Power of Now* and visual symbols of presence hung in my room. Little reminders like, "Stop. Take a Conscious Breath" were scattered in my home. And alas, the Mecca of Tolle followers: attending one of Eckhart and Kim's spiritual retreats, became a goal. In short, my life was devoted to practicing Eckhart Tolle's teachings of living in the Now.

And nothing felt better.

However, time passed. After a few years, something began to happen. I lost that child-like wonder. I noticed myself slipping back into the dreadful conditioning. Instead of feeling my inner body, I threw myself into school and work. Rather than listening to Eckhart Tolle on tape, I blasted music while driving. Instead of feeling my inner body when listening to someone during a conversation, I focused on what I planned to say next. I was no longer reading Tolle's works on a daily basis. I spent my time thinking, mainly about my lack of money, how to make money or finding completion in the future.

In short, I began to feel utter rootedness in Presence was something of the past. Perhaps something I'd lost forever. I wanted it back, but couldn't attain it even though I continued spiritual practices. I began writing.

*   *   *

My experience is the living-reality for many awakened people, or "average spiritual Joes." At this point on the journey, after re-entering the cave, we may feel utterly confused and disheartened. My friend Brian and I often do.

"How did I lose that which was so precious, and most important?" we ask ourselves. We lost what was most meaningful and life-enhancing: our rootedness in presence. (Although of course that dimension is never actually lost, for it is the essence of who we are, as Tolle emphasizes).

As if this sensed loss was not discouraging enough, we began to witness an *increase* in mind activity. In short, we felt as though we failed at being spiritual. Whereas we once lived in an awakened state and had little mind activity, and almost total presence, now an almost non-stop amount of thinking took place. Moreover, these many thoughts demanded us to continually *do* stuff in order to complete our sense of self. Once embedded in the simplicity of the Now, content with what was, our minds resumed their commands to 'get stuff done' and 'make something' of ourselves.

It's totally normal to feel crazier than you ever have felt after awakening. In fact, you may feel that you are more insane than your fellow un-awakened humans. This is because, as Tolle explains, before you woke spiritually, you didn't know you were insane.[7] You didn't even *know* you were constantly thinking. You *were* your mind. After awakening you are present enough to *observe* the crazy thoughts that continuously pass through your mind.

And the insanity only increases. After some time passes post-awakening you will likely begin to feel as though you are fighting to *survive*. And, that is exactly what is happening. Our egos *are* fighting to survive.

See, when you had that initial awakening followed by the span of time you lived your life in presence, the ego in you was temporarily shoved to the back. Consciousness took the driver's seat. The awakening you had literally stunned and silenced your ego. It was as if the awakening put your ego in a coma.

And after a certain amount of time, your conditioned-mind comes out of the coma and wants to rebuild itself, to be stronger than ever! That is why you begin to feel *so* insane. Your ego took a major hit! Now it is redoubled in focus- not only must it rebuild itself, and regain full-strength, it also must make sure the whole awakening thing never happens again.

So you may begin to disregard your spiritual practices as not that important. You may begin to let go of Eckhart Tolle, as I rarely listened to his tapes in my car. And perhaps life and the things of the world once again take center stage.

You could focus on surviving and making something of yourself. You might cling to whatever worldly security you have. Enhancing your social status may become important to you again, or establishing a great career.

Sadly, once you began to lose the total trust in life you developed after your initial awakening you slowly begin to fear life again. And it hurts.

Why? Because you *know* you fear life. Before you awakened and you lived in total fear, you weren't aware that you lived in fear. Knowing that you are living in fear is much more painful than not knowing. But, wait-- hold on: there's a glimmer of hope here! You *know* you live in fear. This means you must still be conscious, or awake to what is going on inside you.

Eckhart Tolle has stated the awakening in you can *never* be reversed.[8] It may lose its importance when the mind takes over, but it can never be stopped altogether. It is powerful to know you are insane. Disheartening yes, but also a very good thing. Because without knowing you are insane, you could *never* be motivated to become fully sane. There actually is a solution- something you can do to put that ego back in a coma for good.

Tolle describes the **pain-body** at length, in both *The Power of Now* and *A New Earth*.[9] For those unfamiliar, the "pain-body" is an entity of pain that lives within you.

It is a negative field of energy comprised of all of the pain you have endured in your life and past life-times as well. Painful situations you did not fully face and accept during your life impede the rootedness within you, and form into a pain-body.

I believe the **most important** instruction Tolle has provided the world with is his description of this daunting entity which rears its ugly head to dominate our lives without us knowing it.

The single most important solution is confronting the pain-body.

Everyone has a pain-body, though some are more dense than others. According to Tolle, anything can trigger the pain-body to come up. For instance, a simple comment made by your partner that was not even meant to inflict pain could trigger your pain-body, and boom- the intense emotion takes the driver-seat; you instantly overreact. You may begin complaining, acting out, condemning those around you, fighting with your partner, or simply thinking negative thoughts. Thus the pain-body has succeeded in dominating you, and creating more pain. In this way, it grows stronger.

For the pain-body to stay alive, Tolle explains, every so often it must take you over and generate more pain so it gets nourished and remains intact. For some individuals, it may be once a week they find themselves caught in a negative mood for hours. The pain-body is regenerating. For others it may be once a month they encounter a situation which triggers the old pain. Tolle says that for some people the pain-body arises daily.

The pain-body may manifest as intense periods of depression. It may present as unbearable bouts of anxiety. In the pain-body, physical symptoms such as stomach-aches may be born, and even illnesses. It is imperative to understand the concept of the pain-body, since it takes control of our beautiful, true selves; it causes problems and chaos, furthering our pain. It destroys qualities of life, work and relationships.[10]

* * *

In *The Power of Now* Tolle says simply being *aware* of the pain-body within us at any given moment is what is necessary in transmuting it:

> *When the pain-body is activated,* know that what you are feeling is the pain-body in you. This knowing is all that is needed to break your identification with it. And when identification with it ceases, the transmutation begins... This means that the pain-body cannot use you anymore and renew itself through you...Not projecting the old emotion into situations means facing it directly within yourself. It may not be pleasant, but it won't kill you. Your Presence is more than capable of containing it. The emotion is not who you are.[11]

In the above words lie the simplicity of Tolle's pain-body practice. All that's required when we feel the pain-body arising is "facing it directly" within ourselves. This means we let ourselves *feel* the pain without resistance, or having to create a mental story around it.

Let it be. Honor the pain within you. It is within you—it isn't you. Don't make an enemy out of it. Know that it is simply old pain that has become activated within you.

Having begun to face the pain-body, we are equipped to call for community, and engage with the growing one which builds the New Earth. The New Earth is a living-reality for humans fully-rooted in Consciousness, not run by thoughts and old pain.

*

How may the pain-body practice free us from mind? How might it bring us back to living in total oneness with life, and awaken us fully, forever?

Well, it's quite simple, actually. What I have decided is that 95% (or more) of what humans do on a daily basis is attempt to avoid feeling pain.

During the time period of my life when I re-entered the cave, I discovered nearly *everything* I did was in order to avoid feeling emotional pain. I lived as a perpetual pain-escaper. Some obvious manifestations were: watching television, listening to music, exercising, socializing, reading, eating, using the internet, cleaning, and doing errands.

But a more subtle method of my pain-escaping phenomenon was my outer-striving for success and completion. Throughout the years I busied myself with getting an education, applying for jobs, working and trying to become someone. I unconsciously did and still do obsess on some of these things, in order to not feel the negative energy of old pain within.

The assumption was that if I "became" someone, through establishing a great career, money or the perfect life- the pain would somehow leave me for good. Yet, after years of running I continue to run, and to no avail. The pain-body within me is still there, no matter what I achieve, no matter what life circumstances.

From little daily things such as surfing the net, watching television or hanging out with friends to the bigger picture things such as developing a career, accumulating a house to live in, or finding a person to marry- the main motivation we all have is to avoid pain.

If humans did not carry a pain-body, daily life would be dramatically different. People would live much more simply. For instance, animals, who do not carry old emotional pain, live quite simple lives. They spend their days being present, taking a nap in the sun, exploring nature, tending to their young, seeking and tending to their shelters, finding food to eat, drinking water alone in silence.

Sure, they must be always on-guard against predators, hunters and dangerous weather conditions. Their reflexes in these situations are superior because their minds are present- not fogged up with emotional pain or concerns about the past, preoccupations with the future. And that's animals in the wild. Domesticated pets often live even more simply, for they have food, water and shelter needs met- so long as their owners take proper care of them. Humans, on the other hand are completely busy, consumed in doing things nearly every minute of the day. And so much of this doing is unnecessary.

This is why I say 95% of what we do is in attempts to escape feeling pain. In fact, a scientific study led by psychologist Timothy Wilson, of the University of Virginia gives a pretty good illustration of what I mean.[12]

Participants were told to sit quietly in a room alone for a range of 6-15 minutes. There would be no cell phones, reading material or anything else in the room. Basically, subjects had to do nothing. Wilson and his colleagues did give the option to push an electric shock button, after which subjects would be allowed to leave the room.

The experimenters were surprised to discover most participants chose to shock themselves rather than simply sit alone for 15 minutes. They left the room.

People would rather endure the physical pain of electric shock than be alone with their pain-body, and no distractions! They will take physical pain over the pain-body.

There are accounts of people who became totally awakened all at once and no longer really did much of anything. They simply sat. Occasionally ate and slept. But mostly they did absolutely nothing. Life was more than enough for them. This of course is an extreme example. However, the way most humans live now is at the opposite <u>extreme</u>. Most people, in order to not feel pain or some sense of incompleteness rush around all day long, and leave no space whatsoever for simply being.

*   *   *

Before awakening 100% of what I did was to avoid feeling the pain-body. Of course at the time I was not aware of it. I lived as a robot, repetitively doing things each day in order to continuously escape the pain I held inside and also, to somehow finally complete myself. Of course this did not work. It only created more pain in my life.

Yet, because I did have that irreversible awakening, 5% of what I do on a daily basis is *not* in attempt to avoid the pain. I say 5% as a rough estimate, of course. Some days it may be more, some days less. But each day I have moments of living fully in the now. Whether it is simply appreciating the beauty of nature, engaging with my pet cat Bayo, conversing on the phone with my friend Brian about present moment living, or sitting alone in the evening in silence and feeling the inner body, or feeling my pain-body consciously for a few minutes...these moments of wakefulness are invaluable and have made me a much happier person overall than I used to be. In fact, it remains those moments of presence that make me truly alive- not the total sleep-walker I was.

*   *   *

Why do we humans have a strong resistance to feeling pain?

Because our minds do not want us to. If we did feel the pain and dissolved it, as Tolle has stated, it would be the end of the ego, or mind, in us.[13] In other words, the ego would die.

We would have very little conditioning left over in us, if the pain-body completely dissolved. The unconscious mind's momentum would be greatly reduced.

Our conditioning is so strong because the pain is there. The challenges of life continuously hit nerves in us, causing us to act out our conditioning, over and over. Yet, if there was no pain within, those "nerves" of ours would not be hit, so to speak.

We would have the ability to choose whether to act out of conditioning or out of presence. It's the pain within that makes us react so quickly when challenged. And what do we act out, so instantly?

Our conditioned responses to pain:

defensiveness, denial, blaming, judging, arguing, sarcasm, acting out of guilt, fear, pride or submission. Escaping what is uncomfortable to us, even if it means we truly suffer more. This is why if the pain-body totally dissolved, if all past pain was forgiven and then let go, or transmuted, as Tolle often says, we would have very little conditioning left.

Leftover conditioning would not be as powerful, nor would it take us over, continuously. If we had no pain at all residing within us, we would be free to do what we actually wanted- to live our lives rooted completely in the Now.

Instead of watching character's lives on a television screen, we would experience life directly- through our own eyes. We would possess forever that child-like wonder, our instincts keen as any wild animal's.

Imagine a world in which human beings did not carry old pain. How different the world would be. It would be the New Earth Tolle invites us to build.

So, do you want to end your ego's existence altogether? Do you want to pull the plug on your conditioned self once and for all? Wanna live freely? As an awakened person? Want actual, permanent enlightenment?

The Buddha said we already have enlightenment. And anyone reading this at times sense it within. Yet, in order to live our lives as enlightened persons, we have to actively, consciously work on transmuting our pain-bodies.

Having gone back and forth in my own pursuit of Consciousness, I see Eckhart Tolle's pain-body practice as the #1 most important practice for anyone to do to become free. Sure, you could practice taking conscious breaths all you want, and attend so many yoga classes that you begin floating above your yoga mat. You can read Tolle's works and listen to his tapes or wear robes like a monk and spend your days at a monastery. You can *try* to live in the present moment every moment. You can throw away all of your possessions and devote your life to living in the here and now. You can give up the big salary and spend everyday consoling the homeless, fostering back to health veterans, the mentally disabled, the recently prison-released. But after a while this won't satisfy you any longer. Because: you *will* remain prisoner to your mind for the rest of your human existence unless and until you deal with the pain-body once, and for all.

Without the pain-body living inside you, weighing you down, you would be free to do anything. You would be free to live in the present moment!

You wouldn't need to perpetually try to find yourself. You would be yourself.

A lot of people who read Tolle's books and practice his teachings are mistaken- they believe the whole pain-body section is just another section, not incredibly important. They may shove it to the side. They believe because they don't blow up on their partners, constantly lie awake nights, get physically violent, cry in their cars or break out in a sweat, shaking in fear, they don't have a pain-body.

But, oh how they are perpetuating their prison-like existences in believing that! News flash- for anyone reading this who is not one hundred percent enlightened: you have a pain-body. Even if its not an extremely heavy one. You have a pain-body, and until you actively practice with it every day, and dissolve it fully you will never be free.

This is only one half of the enlightenment equation. The other half has to do with community. Besides rare individuals such as the Buddha, Tolle, Jesus, Mohammed, Byron Katie etc., for the most part we humans are not strong enough to become enlightened on our own, to get through the pain alone.

Just like Plato's cave dwellers, the majority of humans are unable to face their pain alone, to break free of their chains. We need to come together and form a Global Community, which will be discussed later in this book.

*

The emphasis on transmuting the pain-body is not meant to disregard the other present-moment practices, or "portals"[13] Tolle gives us. Such practices must be used in tandem with the pain-body exercise. All ways we employ discipline and encourage serenity aid the process of awakening fully. Only once you transmute some of your personal pain are you able to fully engage in such practices.

AVOIDING THE PAIN
STARTS IN CHILDHOOD

Think how parents and other adults speak to their children. Statements such as, "Look at the beautiful art work you made in school today!." Or, "you need to go outside and play." Now, you may be wondering what is wrong with such statements.

In and of themselves, there's absolutely nothing *wrong* with those statements. But, as Tolle has said, even the most innocent thing in the world, when used in *excess*- or repeatedly can turn into something which is destructive, or life-diminishing. Here's how.

Eckhart Tolle says incessantly commenting on, or otherwise harping on your child's existence leaves no room for silence. For you or for the child. It breeds ego and mind.[14] He explains the child quickly learns to not only become *uncomfortable* with silence, but also adapts to focus *solely* on the world of form. This creates dysfunction.

The child, who was once rooted totally in Presence literally *forms* into an egoic human. The child loses utter innocence while they are taught, unconsciously by adults, to see the outside world as the only thing that matters. Tolle emphasizes this in *A New Earth*.

Because parents place such heavy importance on diagnosing, mentioning, reacting to every little thing that goes on in the child's life- the child begins to live from "object-consciousness" as Tolle describes. Or, in other words, having one's primary focus on the things of this world, and having no inner space awareness whatsoever.[15]

This is the beginning of human conditioning, Tolle tells us. It starts at a young age. And it is unfortunate for the child because of course he or she has no say in the matter. The parents micro-manage the child's very existence, by constantly commenting on what goes on and incessantly telling the child what to do.

In this way, the child is robbed of the opportunity to explore the world on their own. Now, of course, the parents do not realize they are hurting their child. They believe they are enhancing their child's life when they provide their child with non-stop stimuli, activities and attention. No one would intentionally, or consciously hurt their own child as Tolle would say.[15]

Sadly, many kids receive their conditioning from technology. Some parents simply to put food on the table must resort to letting the TV keep an eye on their child while they work or take care of things around the house. Or they give the child an assortment of digital distractions: hand-held game systems, cell phones, computers and tablets.

Children often spend hours a day playing video games. Here, the conditioning is electronic and happens even quicker. As Tolle describes, the child loses his or her ability to pay attention to anything for long because on the screen everything happens instantly. With each press of a button there is an immediate result, change, distraction from one moment to the next. Beats sitting in a room, doing nothing, correct? Beats the electric shock- and its cousin, the pain-body. Well, it feels better, anyway, which is why the child picks up so quickly on it, and thereafter constantly wants new derivations.

This is dangerous because the child will grow up expecting that his or her needs are met immediately. And this is not the case in the real world. Allowing your child to spend hours each day using electronics is, in a sense, turning your child into a robot.

What's also unfair is that parents unknowingly promote the growth of their children's pain-body.[16] For instance, when the child falls and scrapes his or her knee, the parent usually rushes in with a panic, grabs the child and exclaims in an excited voice, "are you okay?!?" This reaction is followed by immediately bandaging the cut and often the child is given a piece of candy to make everything better.

Of course you should attend to your child when he or she hurts themselves in a fall. But instead of making the sole focus the fall, and instantly making things better, take a moment of silence after your child scrapes his or her knee.

Honor the moment. Watch how the child reacts. Without the parent's extreme reaction, the child may actually be just fine. Then, after giving your child alert, silent attention, which is what they truly *need*, as Tolle points out,[17] take care of your child's injury.

In this way you allow the child to *face* their pain without running from it. This is a tremendous lesson and an extremely important one for your child to learn. In fact, Tolle states that in any pain the child endures, whether physical or emotional, it is important you honor the child's pain and help him or her to do the same.

Because remember, conditioning starts in childhood. If the child is taught to immediately escape their pain and fix it with

TV-watching, an i-pad or a cookie, this will extend into adulthood.

Indeed we are living in a world in which adults who are unable to face their pain teach their children to avoid pain. Addictions form at a much younger age than you may think. Teaching your child to be in the moment with the pain and not immediately try to escape from it, fix it or divert their attention elsewhere is the single most important thing you could ever teach your child.

*

Bullying is a widespread phenomenon these days as the collective human mind becomes more dysfunctional. When a child bullies another, this is a form of the young perpetrator's pain-body creating more pain, and thus feeding and growing stronger. If your child is the one bullying, he or she may be avoiding, or distracting themselves from their pain by causing another's.

However, for both the bully and the child being bullied, this is very painful. Tolle has said "pain-bodies can mutually energize each other."[18] The victim of bullying experiences emotional pain and this in turn feeds his or her growing pain-body. The bully acts out in order to lessen his or her own pain, which only causes them more pain in the end.

In order to prevent your child's pain-body from growing at each emotional trauma, it is important to be the space for the child when you notice they are suffering, suggests Tolle. Whether the child opens up to you about the bullying or not, it is so important to *be there*.

Try not to let your own pain-body creep up and explode in anger. It is not necessary to be upset because your child has been hurt. He or she will be hurt many more times. Set a precedent. Give your child the best example you can: be the space and allow your child's pain, as well as your own, to be.

In this way you are not feeding the child's pain or victim identity with endless comments about the situation, which only makes the situation more real for your child's growing ego.

How is it possible to "be the space" for your child's pain? Tolle says it requires being fully alert and present- not lost in thinking, or emotions. Your presence alone, if it is strong enough, will help the child dissolve the pain they are feeling and thus prevent their pain-body from growing. Your calm and centeredness is contagious, especially to someone as mutable and susceptible as a child. The pain-body cannot exist in your presence. This is illustrated with Tolle's words: "The pain-body…is actually afraid of the light of your consciousness."[19]

Eckhart Tolle discusses all of this in *A New Earth*. I bring it up because it is so important to prevent the collective human pain-body from growing. But, as Tolle would likely say, before you can help your child in this process, you must be the space for your own pain first.

THE MOST IMPORTANT TASK OF ADULTHOOD / DISTRACTIONS FROM THE PAIN

As adults we have been so thoroughly conditioned. Typically we maintain a complete outer-reality focus. When anything goes "wrong," like when a child scrapes his or her knee, we instantly use objects to fix it. We pick up the phone and call a friend, in hopes they will make our pain go away, or we crack open a beer, or pour ourselves a glass of wine to dull the pain, and numb the anxiety we feel. The candy or ice cream our parents gave us as children to make us feel better when we encountered pain turns into other forms of pleasure-seeking, and even addictions, in our 20's.

Man-made society, and everything it encompasses is created by the ego in an attempt to distract us from feeling the pain within. Apart from the natural world of course, everything is hand-crafted by the ego to keep us focused outward, and thus keep the ego alive.

Yes, even your career was created in order to distract you. In fact, working is one of the *main* pain-body distractions. You wake up, get ready for work, drive, take a bus or otherwise get yourself to your work place, put in your hours and drive home. But, you're not necessarily finished once you arrive home. You make dinner for yourself or your family, clean up, and otherwise attend to your needs and responsibilities.

But you may also make a meal to take to your next shift, or set out your clothes for the next day, prepare the coffee-maker for the morning, set the alarm and so on, all in a kind of mental preparation of work the next day. You may spend time on work when you are at home: paperwork, research, checking emails. Simply *thinking* about tomorrow's work is a form of work. Stressing about work is labor.

You may work extra shifts or rarely take a holiday. Even as children, when we are in school, our parents and teachers tell us to study hard so we can have a good career. Preparation for work keeps young people- who are not yet chained to a job distracted from pain. Large sums of money are paid for tuition. Much time is devoted to learning and studying to earn a degree, or learn a trade so we can work and thus distract ourselves from pain. Mad isn't it? as Eckhart might say.

How else does the world as we know it present itself as one giant distraction? Well apart from work and the huge amount of attention given to making money, keeping afloat, managing bills and mortgages, accumulating more money, saving for retirement, perhaps living with the pressures of surmounting debt or bankruptcy, spending money to let others know how much money you have- there's the social aspect.

The social life is another tremendous distraction from feeling the pain-body within you. People devote a lot of time to "having a life." Having the right friends and going to the right events. We pay money to maintain this social life, to be able to engage, find a suitor, impress, feel part of something, make connections, further your career or simply to fit in. To not feel lonely, or have to be alone with ourselves. If we don't continually engage we may feel we don't matter. It is great lengths we go to, just to distract ourselves from the pain.

It is great to enjoy time with friends and develop or foster strong, healthy, lasting relationships. And, as the world stands, we need money to provide ourselves and our dependents with food and shelter. To work and engage are necessary and healthy activities. However, it is important to realize careers and social lives can and often do stand as major distractions from the pain.

They may suck us in so deeply, and take so much of our energy that there's little left for spiritual practice, let alone sitting with the pain-body and transmuting it.

The social clubs, restaurants and bars, the alcohol served at such places, the mostly ego-feeding music played are examples of how the societal ego creates more and more "stuff" to keep itself intact.

Romantic relationships and marriage can be distractions. Churches, temples and mosques can be. Clubs, athletics, workshops, yoga classes- nearly anything, whether or not is healthy, can serve as ways we busy ourselves or otherwise escape pain. By doing a self-inventory, we can discover whether we are filling or emptying our minds.

Having children is another major form of unconscious diversion from facing the pain-body. Many people subconsciously assume if they have children, this will free them from the pain inside: loneliness, fear, a sense of incompleteness, a need to please a parent, a fear of a deteriorating marriage, anger, sadness or what have you. But it won't.

Having children is rewarding, but also distracts- it is not easy and often creates further pain. If you have been using your children to keep the pain from rising up totally, just sit with that. If you have been using your partner or spouse in this way, let that sink in.

Awareness is what is most important, as Tolle states. With awareness you are free from using familial duties as a distraction from the pain. Instead, you can allow yourself to feel the pain, which teaches your children to do the same. Your own awareness may motivate your significant other.

Moreover, if relationships or family dynamics cause you pain, such as sleep-deprivation, frustration, etc., use it to practice transmuting your pain-body. For Tolle states that, "even the slightest irritation is significant and needs to be acknowledged and looked at; otherwise, there will be a cumulative buildup of unobserved reactions."[20]

Tolle and other spiritual teachers tell us the world improves and gets worse simultaneously. We can see this when viewing the world in terms of pain-body distraction.

The world becomes more imbued with spiritual language and phenomenon. Recently yoga and Reiki, ancient and new-age practices are extremely popular. Books such as Tolle's *The Power of Now*, Byron Katie's *The Work*, and the writings of Ram Dass, Thich Nhat Han and the Dali Lama are world-wide best sellers. Spiritual retreats and centers are more common. One could say there is a wide-spread spiritual evolution occurring on the planet right now.

And the ego is terrified by this- hence, the world also appears crazier than ever. The ego, in attempts to keep us from going into the pain and thus removing the ego completely, has recently created an array of new distraction devices.

It is as if there is more "stuff" than ever before to steal our attention. This new stuff ranges from material goods, foods and other ingredients to try- even new types of water to drink. Movies and other media get more complex and often more graphic. Video games, music and electronic gadgets are popular ways people kill time rather than be it.

Fads like electronic bracelets constantly monitor how many steps people take each day, and how many hours of sleep they get. Smart watches attach information to our wrists. Such gadgets are useful but when used in excess distract us from what really matters, *the now*. Healthy devices intended to make us more functional easily become dysfunctional.

Billboards, advertisements, notifications on our gadgets signaling and chiming- can you see here, how the ego is quite successful in creating a world in which we don't have to feel pain? It creates all we need to escape easily.

No matter if it is something essential as a phone, whether it is educational or down-right pornographic- media and devices are departures from the Now. And we are bombarding ourselves with information. Why do we want to escape the perfect Now?

*   *   *

It's common to feel frustrated waiting in line or sitting in traffic, or waiting rooms. Why do we get frustrated when waiting? People seek constant distraction. From themselves. From the pain that lies within them.

In the car we may use the radio or phone to avoid silence. After all, the alternative may be sitting at a red light, alone with the pain-body.

Doctor's offices provide magazines. Otherwise it would be a waiting room full of pain-bodies.

*

Recently I went to my dentist. An elderly woman was in the waiting room. Her husband had just been called in to get his teeth taken care of. It was just me and this woman for about 25 minutes in the small room. I used the waiting room experience as a sort of meditation. In this state I felt a slight vibration of negative energy within. The pain-body.

I sat with it for some time. Simultaneously, I observed the woman and could tell she was fighting against her own pain-body. She rapidly flipped through magazines, until that no longer worked. Then she began a series of unnecessary behaviors: fixed her hair, adjusted the straps on her purse, organized things within it, got up, stretched her arms and legs, went to the bathroom, came back and even walked around the waiting room, looking closely at the oral health posters on the walls.

The woman had a slight frown on her face as she did all this- a seriousness. Saying hello to me, or looking in my eyes was out of the question. She glanced at me a couple times but then immediately fidgeted with her purse, or otherwise remained disengaged. A stark realization came over me: that will be me if I don't continue to sit with the pain-body in my daily life.

I looked at the woman and pondered what she may have looked like as a child. In fact, I saw her as a child that was dealt unnecessary pain by others and now finds it impossible to sit still while waiting at the dentist.

This woman represents all of us. So next time you go to the dentist or doctor's office, experiment with how it feels to do nothing. Don't even bring your phone into the waiting room. See if you discover pain, even the slightest *tension* within. Notice others around you- are they taking advantage of the quiet, and the opportunity to do nothing? Or are they acting as the woman did- trying desperately to avoid stillness. We are each other's mirrors. We are not here to judge, but we may glean very much about ourselves by quietly observing others.

As I am writing it occurs to me a lot of people keep reading material in their bathrooms. We've become a society that cannot use the bathroom without distraction. Can you imagine a cat using the litter box while also flipping through a magazine?

*   *   *

If you open your eyes it is easy to see ways the collective human ego increases in destruction. Violent crime and mass-shootings are unceasing. Obesity rises. Heroin and pharmaceutical drug-abuse is at a dangerous high. Women's rights are being attacked, and their civil liberties threatened. Black people are murdered, not having committed crimes. News outlets do their best to distract us with fluff pieces since without breaks, the destruction may be too uncomfy to bear!

We spend less and less time outside and more time receiving information. The ego creates perfect distractions: Facebook, Instagram, Snapchat, Twitter, Pinterest—it is a growing list which perpetually removes our attention from what matters the most: the Now and everything in it, including residual pain.

It's sad and almost humorous at the same time to see how humans spend so much of our time posting what we are doing on Twitter, rather than paying quality attention to what we are doing. Social media addiction is one of the ego's biggest distractions from the Now. News channels, particular crimes or events or political races and the like have a very addictive quality; people just can't stop checking in.

Notice the many ways the mind traps us in perpetual distraction.

MAKE A FULL COMMITMENT TO CONSCIOUSNESS

Many spiritual practices help bring us into the now and make us feel good- temporarily. The pain will return, continuously taking us over. Therefore, we need to devote our entire spiritual practice to transmuting the pain-body. "The best way out, is always through."[21]

The good news is, we don't have to go anywhere or pay a fee to work with the pain-body. We can do it at home in our pajamas any time of the day.

Try it. Right now. Go into your body and become still. Make the pain your sole attention. Breathe, and feel the pain. Note the way the body feels, then feel the emotion. Let the pain be there. Be present with it. This is the most crucial undertaking.

Sometimes when I sense negative energy within, I use visualization. I picture inside my body a tiny version of myself tied to a rope. I watch the rope slowly descend further down into my being. The more I descend, the deeper the pain I feel.

I allow myself to merge into the darkness within until the pain nearly overwhelms me. Try this. Allow yourself to go deeper and deeper into the pain within, until you see yourself totally surrounded by darkness.

You may feel as though you can't breathe. You may even feel slightly sick. Stay with the sickness. Breathe and hold the negative energy. You will find the darkness turns to light. The pain that was trapped is now freed. Each time we do this, the amount of time free from pain increases. Each time we come back to face the pain, we do so having been fortified from the last time we faced it.

It doesn't take a death in the family, or a foreclosed home to trigger your pain-body. It could be waiting at the dentist's, and feeling negative energy as the woman and I did. If you get frustrated, that's old pain coming up. If you are in a bad mood or are having a "bad day," that is pain-body rising up, making you feel that way, Tolle says.[22]

Make a plan to sit with it. If you recognize yourself as fed-up or antsy, if something someone says or does makes you feel negative- make an appointment with yourself to sit with it, for that is the only thing that will *truly* free you.

CHAPTER THREE

GIVE UP ATTACHMENT TO YOUR TEACHER

Imagine a grad school student who shows up for every lecture, pays full attention in class, studies hard and graduates with honors. The student may truly appreciate his professors for supplying what was necessary for earning that degree. Even so, it is highly doubtful that after graduation, the student constantly thinks about his old professors or compares himself to them.

The same goes for you on the spiritual journey. Yes, life presented immense pain and obstacles. It then provided you with the works of someone like Eckhart Tolle. The teachings in *The Power of Now* or *A New Earth* outlined everything you needed to learn, or to realize within yourself. It was monumental and changed your entire outlook on life. Yet, like the graduate student, you've already graduated. You have become awake to who you truly are. For this Tolle's books were immensely helpful, even necessary. So be thankful to Tolle, but don't cling to him. If you do, you could end up constantly comparing yourself to him.

You may start to think, "Eckhart Tolle wouldn't have done what I just did," after arguing with a co-worker, or ignoring your children. Some Christians wear the famous W.W.J.D. bracelets.

Becoming too attached to one's spiritual teacher is a trap. Personally, when trying to live up to Eckhart Tolle, I've ended up with feelings of guilt: I couldn't measure up. Here, it is easy to see that comparing yourself to your spiritual teacher will only make you feel like a failure and keep you stuck in ego.

Tolle and other spiritual masters had unique journeys perfect for them- not necessarily for you. So, instead of focusing on the teacher, give more attention to the teaching itself, within you. *Within you*? What does that mean?

Well, after reading Tolle's works, begin to live them. Feel your own presence as you go about your day. If you witness yourself operating under the influence of the ego, simply hold awareness of that- but don't mentally berate yourself for falling short of Tolle, regardless how many years you've spent reading his books, practicing Presence. Eckhart Tolle was *supposed* to awaken all at once as he did. And apparently, you were *not* supposed to. Why? Because you didn't. Tolle often recites these famous words from the poet Hafiz:

> I am a hole in a flute
> that the Christ's breath
> moves through.
> Listen to this music!

"Christ" can represent Consciousness, or Life itself. When you are open to Life it will work through you and indeed play a beautiful, unique note. Thus, instead of listening only to Eckhart Tolle or some other spiritual teacher's note, be aware that you too are "a hole in the flute;" an integral part of the One. You are just as important Tolle, Jesus, the Buddha and so on. You will know this as you listen to the music within yourself.

WORSHIPPING: IS IT STILL NECESSARY?

Letting go of attachment to one's spiritual teacher or religion can be freeing. Although I was raised Catholic, at one point in my life I felt Christianity, or any religion for that matter, actually served as an obstacle for me in fully connecting to Consciousness. I saw how religion focused primarily on concepts. Or in other words, it centered around thoughts rather than essence. The recitations and prayers lost all meaning for me. Worshiping someone or something *outside myself* contradicted my own rootedness in Being.

When you know yourself as being one with Life, or rather when you know that you *are* Life itself, worshiping another can become idolatry, and in a way it begins to feel silly. I knew deep down Jesus did not desire to be worshiped- as an idol. He broke bread with the rich, poor, criminals and tax collectors. He did not see himself as superior to anyone. He taught us we are all one, under God. Therefore, I let go of my Catholic identity. I felt liberated- no longer absorbed in utter devotion to someone outside me.

*

I now more deeply appreciate Jesus' many teachings. Whereas when practicing Catholicism, I did not understand their deeper, truer meaning, after reading Tolle, I see Jesus' parables and the like in a whole different light. I see true words of enlightenment.

I now realize, as Tolle points out, Jesus' words on being connected to the vine and thus bearing fruit is a symbolization of being rooted in Consciousness. Only when we are in touch with who we really *are* can we authentically bring about fruitfulness in life.[2]

Just as leaving Catholicism freed me, dropping one's total identification with Tolle can be rewarding. In fact, I believe it to be necessary.

Brian and I independently reached a point where we had to publicly denounce Tolle. This happened during complete hopelessness and disheartenment. Our identification with Tolle, comparing ourselves to him became too heavy for us, and frustrating. We praised, glorified and loved Tolle- and suddenly disdained him since we knew subconsciously trying to be like him was futile. So focused on Tolle, Brian and I felt we were missing vital signs along the paths of our personal journeys.

Tolle's works are invaluable and still very helpful to me on a daily basis, but I no longer compare myself to him or see him as someone to eventually become.

It is important to remain confident in our own paths, which require our full attention. Even if we feel we constantly mess up, spiritually-speaking, we can't really mess up on the journey of awakening, because as Eckhart Tolle states, "All that is cannot be otherwise."[3]

Like many, you may glorify Tolle- seeing him almost as a god, in the same way teenagers get lost worshiping pop stars as idols. The way the retreat-goers lost themselves when they rushed to the stage, to take pictures.

Getting "lost" in worship gives worship a negative connotation. However, in the early stages of a spiritual journey, worship can be a positive, even necessary part of awakening.

Embedded in worship is recognition of the Good. Specifically, when worshipping someone like Tolle or Jesus, what you are really worshipping is the Good you see in them. But at some point, you must renounce your attachment to worshiping people outside of yourself. You must discover what is already stated in the Bible: "Be Still and Know that I Am God."[4] You must know yourself as God. Just as you must let go of pain and thus ego, it is time to let go of worship and be aware of the Good in you.

There is nothing wrong with religion in and of itself. Religion serves as a positive emotional outlet and spiritual practice for many. However, when practicing religion, it is important to be aware of the divine within *yourself*, rather than merely focusing on a person outside you.

During Catholic mass the congregation says together, "Lord, I am not worthy that you should enter under my roof, but only say the word and my soul shall be healed."[5] Post-awakening I simply wouldn't say that line, at mass. I found the words contradictory. How can anyone's soul be healed? Your soul is the most precious thing on this earth- it is the divine within you. Since we are divine, in and of ourselves we do not need healing. Our mind creates the suffering.

Religion perpetuates the idea we are inherently bad, or "unworthy." In this way it has control over its followers, keeping them trapped in ego. Ego wants you to believe that you are bad, that there is something wrong with who you are. Because then, as Tolle explains, the ego is strengthened. It stays alive. If you don't have a problem with who you are, you are free to simply be you. This is why the Buddhist Master said,

No self, no problem.

WHAT PREVENTS YOU FROM LIVING LIKE ECKHART TOLLE?

It is important to see that Tolle, Jesus and the Buddha are innately no different from you. They and others like them were able to access the gold that we all sit on. Tolle gave us this metaphor, in the Preface of *The Power of Now*.[6]

A beggar sits on what he thinks is an old, empty box. He'd been sitting on it his whole miserable life. A stranger walks by and tells the poor beggar to look inside. When he does, he discovers the box is full of gold. We already have all we need within us; we are already enlightened.

Yet we are often trapped as beggars, while Tolle has complete access to the gold at all times. Why are we the beggar and he a rich man? It's simple, really. He underwent a radical, overnight awakening. He awoke one morning and had no ego whatsoever, and an 80% reduction in thinking.

Amazing! But pay attention to what came before the awakening: Tolle lived with extreme anxiety and suicidal depression until the age of twenty-nine. One dark night an immense, overwhelming, all-encompassing flood of pain overcame him. Tolle experienced a pain so great that on an emotional level it likely paralleled Jesus' crucifixion.

Before he awoke, and indeed, this is likely what caused him to become enlightened- *all* of Eckhart's pain-body came up at once. And he faced it. Head-on. Tolle[7] heard a voice say, "resist nothing" so he didn't fight the pain. He fell asleep, woke up, and boom, totally awakened. Permanent shift.

The way to awakening is through facing the pain-body and totally accepting it.

There are accounts of Jesus going to the desert for 40 days and encountering "the devil."[8] The devil was Jesus' own mind and corresponding pain-body. He had the courage to be completely alone and face his pain and thus came out of the desert enlightened.

In fact, after his experience in the desert is when Jesus' ministry began, according to the Bible. It was following the desert experience that Jesus began to teach, adopt disciples and perform miracles.

His solo journey of sitting for 40 days with his pain-body and ego nearly destroyed him, but left him enlightened. Later in the New Testament comes the famous account of his transfiguration.[9] It describes how Jesus appeared to be filled and surrounded with a white light. Tolle often describes how people who have become awake appear to have a light as though projected from within. The heavy, dense self and negative energy of the pain-body no longer reside in them.

Another example of retreat to the wild is spiritual author and teacher, Byron Katie. After years of being extremely depressed and suicidal she had a spontaneous awakening. Immediately after, she went into the desert alone. Katie "spent a lot of time in the desert…just listening."[10] She would listen to the stories in her mind. She knew these stories were not reality, nor who we are. In the desert she found the influential "Work," the four questions which have helped many step out of the crazy stream of thinking.

Up to this point in the evolution of Consciousness, going alone into the desert is one major way to become fully awake to our true essence. Whether we literally travel to one, or whether we sit alone in our room at night and allow ourselves to be overtaken by the pain-body without offering resistance: at some point, we all must endure the pain we've run from since birth.

Most of us are unable to fully face the pain alone. It seems too terrifying. Trekking to the desert to fully dissolve pain became a goal for Brian and me. Over long phone calls we entertained the idea of Death Valley, California. We could go for a week to simply sit in our separate silences, in the utter wild. Brian even paid for a car rental for 6 months in advance for us to do this! Yet, as time went on, somehow our desert plans were no longer necessary.

For me, this happened after 8 months of applying to jobs, and going to interviews. Zero job offers later, I became depressed. I was stuck in the mind and thus did not trust in the universe's plans for me. With no job and no job offers I experienced my own, natural desert period. It was the wasteland in me, and one I helped create. Many fantasize having so much free time would be wonderful. The truth is, having so much empty time leads to a major lack of distractions and that unresolved pain-body will hit you like a Semi-Truck.

My ego spent that "free" time worrying about future. Thoughts such as "what if I never get a job," flooded my mind. No job or prospects, I felt like a meaningless failure. I lived in my mother's house, though I was grown. The "story of me" became one giant mistake.

Even though I earned my bachelor's degree a year before, I felt as though I had accomplished nothing in life. My hold on spirituality went out the window. My mind created more and more poor-me thoughts and fear thoughts, which led to anxiety and depression. I even stopped talking to Brian during this time. The pain got so severe that I became extremely suicidal.

I even banged my head against a wall, in sheer lunacy. This resulted in a bump on my forehead. The bump reminded me when I saw it: I am out of control. My pain was at an all-time high. I was in the desert and I couldn't escape. There was no electric shock button to press. I hit absolute rock bottom. Nearly every thought I had was to somehow no longer exist. Driving home late one night I parked my car by an empty field. Something told me to do this- even though it was a very cold fall night. I went to the middle of the field. I sat down and cried. Then I stopped crying and laid down. I looked up at the stars, for it was a clear sky. I surrendered to it.

Somehow, I went into the pain-body. I avoided doing so for four weeks out of fear. I guess the pain was so bad, I had no other option but to face it. I let myself feel it, while refraining from any thoughts of being killed or dying.

Laying there on the field, under the stars I felt a silence. The pain led to a stillness. In that moment I knew everything was going to be okay. In fact, everything had been okay. It always is. My attitude, my perspective had taken me over. I fed the ego, and did it relentlessly. Under the stars I knew even my relentless ego-feeding was exactly as it should be.

I got up and went home.

My partner came over the next day, after we had been apart ten days. When I saw her I started bawling. It was the comfort of seeing her face that made me cry. I had denied myself this comfort, while feeding the ego. Each day I felt a bit better.

That weekend I attended a Reiki attunement class my mom arranged for me. After the class I felt joy again. It felt good to be alive. I started seeing the beauty of life once again, in the little things all around. I was still very unsure where life was taking me but I allowed that un-knowing to be. Having faced the pain, I was much more receptive to what went on at the class. It strengthened me. And I knew I'd keep on strengthening.

Resisting where I was in life was what made me suffer most. I began to actually trust in life again. I trusted myself. I let go of the need to control, and accepted my "life situation," as Eckhart would call it.

After this psychological desert, I came out a bit lighter. I am now grateful for the trials I faced, for what came next was action- including true plans for writing this book. I knew it was time to devote myself to building the New Earth. Eckhart Tolle describes such an experience as I had perfectly:

> There's nothing more beautiful in life, than a failed story."

If you are going through a desert period in your life, keep going. Whether psychological or physical in nature, deserts are what enable many people to trust life with abandon. The only way to live fully in the present moment is to have that trust in life. Without it you will worry about the future, and what it may bring, or regret the path you took in the past.

When the New Earth is a living reality it is very likely we will no longer need to go through suicidal pain or depression. With support of a community, it will be easier to stay present in the here and now- where "there are no problems," as Tolle states,[12] and trust in life will be the most *natural* thing.

Surrounded by conscious people, it is natural to become conscious yourself. In the mean time, endure your desert periods. Learn from them; trust Life to support you.

LET GO OF THE SPIRITUAL IDENTIFICATION YOU CLING TO

No spiritual practice will work for you long, unless you transmute your pain-body into Presence. That is why so many people become very passionate about Tolle's teachings but leave the teachings behind, after time.

You may read the latest Thich Nhat Hahn book and become very passionate about breathing mindfully. A few weeks later- where is that mindful breathing? It was, of course sabotaged by the pain that was always there, under the surface.

Spirituality itself, or the seeking of it can become an addiction, a form of escape that works for a while. But it typically goes out of the window when it is no longer effective in masking the pain. If you practice the mindful breathing while periodically facing the pain-body, it won't wear off.

I've always thought I must be crazy, or a spiritual failure. Now, thoroughly devoted to a spiritual teaching, then- boom! Behaving in ways that oppose the teaching. I was confused. I could not understand why I loved the teachings of Eckhart Tolle, practiced them authentically and experienced the bliss of oneness with Life, yet slowly but surely returned to continuous thinking. Even after years of practice, either my mind or pain-body showed up, like an old friend that won't leave.

Some may read *A New Earth*, realize its truth deep within but then two weeks later, somehow want nothing to do with it. Others may practice Tolle's teachings for a decade after reading his works. But then, the egoic mind creeps up again. They may begin behaving in unhealthy ways, or thinking again at rapid speed. Any of us could become apathetic enough to leave *The Power of Now* on the shelf. We lose Consciousness.

The reason you picked up this book is because this phenomenon is true for you. You wouldn't be reading this book if you were totally free of pain and ego. If Eckhart Tolle's wonderful teachings had truly *worked* for you, it is likely you would not have this book in your hands right now.

Why did you love Eckhart Tolle's teachings after first reading them? Deep within, the Consciousness that you *are* recognized the truth of his words. The truth behind Tolle is the truth that lives within you, that *is you*. To recognize this is beautiful. It demonstrates that we are all one. You are no different from Tolle on the level of Being.

The difference is Tolle doesn't have an egoic mind- we do. Before he wrote *The Power of Now*, his pain-body dissolved. This is why he is able to successfully practice his own teachings. This is why he is able to stay in the inner body most of the day, whereas you or I are not. This is why he lives fully in the now with no concern for past or future, while we ruminate.

We must accept that we have not yet had—and maybe never will—an overnight awakening as Tolle did, and that this is okay. We shouldn't identify as failures, however, for this not only adds to our pain-body, but also leads to a more crystallized sense of self as Tolle explains.[13] Pain-body and the ego are two sides of a coin. They are one. The pain-body is "the dark shadow cast by the ego."[14] Which means if you have yet to transmute your pain-body, you have an egoic mind. These sabotage attempts to fully awaken, every time.

But when you dissolve the pain-body, you take the ego down with it. When your pain-body is gone, you will be able to practice Tolle's teachings successfully. In fact you won't even need a spiritual practice anymore. You will live it.

And it will be easy. No effort will be required to live in the Now. It will be the most natural thing. Just as a famous guitar player no longer needs to take guitar lessons. You will no longer need to meditate. Life will be a constant meditation.

When you begin facing your pain with no distractions, it may overwhelm you. You may lie down in your room in the fetal position with tears streaming down your face. Or you may have a headache or stomach ache when facing your pain. Walk through the gates of hell: embrace your pain and truly feel it.[15]

The good news is, the more and more you sit with your pain it may actually start to feel good. Sometimes, when my pain-body has been triggered, I sit with it. At first it feels uncomfortable, and downright painful.

When I stay with the pain, I soon begin to discover within myself that I am one with that pain. I believe it begins to feel good because the pain merges with Consciousness.

Like ice returns to gas or liquid form, pain returns to its original state: life energy. Eckhart Tolle says that everything is life energy, including the pain! He states that the pain-body is made up of life energy that was blocked in your body because you were unable to face it when the painful happening originally occurred.[16]

Thus, the pain is not some menacing, terrible thing to be fought against. It is life energy, innocently trapped.

Turn it into good energy. Become the miner. Seams open. The coal becomes the diamond.

CHAPTER FOUR

INNER-CHANGE →
OUTER-CHANGE

OUTER-CHANGE →
INNER-CHANGE

Think back to your initial awakening. For a few moments close your eyes and remember what happened during that precious time in your human existence.

Remember how things changed, and more importantly, how you *felt* as you lived on this earth as an awakened being. How did the way you live change?

For anyone who has experienced any sort of awakening from utter mind identification, some transformation must have occurred. It could be that your eyes displayed a brightness that was not there before. Or maybe you ditched your TV-watching habit at night and instead went for a long evening walk.

It may be post-awakening you treated your body better. Or maybe you didn't. But, it's almost a guarantee that after realizing the true, profound nature of your existence, at least one positive change occurred. Because, as Eckhart Tolle states, your inner state and outer reality are completely "inter-twined".[1]

When something inside undergoes change, it leads to an outer shift. In the case of waking up spiritually, this change is always a good thing. Inner change → Outer change. When you let go of the heavy, false sense of self, you have more space inside, Tolle explains.[2] And this space is reflected in your outer reality.

Perhaps after awakening to who you really are, you trust your intuition and live a life you've never imagined. When it happened to me, I shifted focus from school and career to a more simple life with more time for reflection, and ample time for pain-body practice. This wasn't something I had control over or truly understood. I followed my feelings. If something felt terrible, I dropped it. Otherwise, why do it?

Only through following your intuition and trusting your feelings are you living aligned with the universe and its plans for you. Each step of the journey, whether painful or pleasant, is necessary and part of the whole.

The Buddha stated, "What you think, you become. What you feel, you attract. What you imagine, you create." Post-awakening you are more likely to attract and be attracted to people, activities and environments which are conducive to living fully aware in the present.

You may be able to share your own story of how awakening your inner-being transformed your outer-world. And it would be a beautiful story- after all, it's a miracle. Can you imagine resuming the life you led pre-awakening? I certainly could not.

However, if you are not fully enlightened there is ego in you. You act, speak and think like an insane human at times. Don't worry, I do too, and that is why I'm writing this book!

Eckhart Tolle states, "If you get the inside right, the outside will fall into place."[3] These beautiful words point to an even more wondrous reality. Anyone can see how they ring true for Tolle. While many who walk the planet spend their time in the same unconscious environment, year after year, Tolle doesn't have to. He travels the world to speak to his large fan-base. Tolle's "career" is a direct manifestation of his inner-reality. A reality of total trust in the universe. Tolle has no need to feel secure by having all the right circumstances. He lives totally in the now, and comes in contact with what the present moment offers: beauty, true love and abundance.

Lets look at the Buddha's words as they regard Tolle:

What you feel, you attract.

He attracted Kim Eng, who is a totally awesome, free-spirited partner with values that line up with his. Tolle created three life-changing books.

What you imagine, you create.

All of Tolle's books have helped transform people's lives; they began spiritual-awakening on a global scale. Moreover, Eckhart Tolle is loved.

If you've ever been to a retreat of his, or watched one of his lectures online, you can see the audience loves him. His light-hearted spiritual humor is enough to make the grumpiest of men smile. His body-language and demeanor are enough to make a teen put down a cell phone, and return to the Now.

Tolle spreads love and receives love, wherever he goes. It's that simple. Because Tolle does what he loves, and believes in on a daily basis. He is living his truth. And the universe supports him fully in that endeavor, as it supports us when we do what we love.

There is true human connection he and Kim share with millions of people who appreciate the Truth. How connected do you feel? Are you doing what you really want to be doing on a daily basis?

Are you living the Truth you so deeply resonate with when reading the *The Power of Now*? Moreover, do you live primarily from fear, or from trust? These are important questions.

Doing what you were born to do is extremely important. It will determine how you feel and how your life unfolds. Spiritual teacher and author Osho illustrates this beautifully with a story about a musician and his father in India.

According to the story, the man's father desperately wants him to be a doctor. The father insists if he follows his dream of being a musician, he will starve. When the man attends a music university instead of medical school, he is disowned by his whole family.

Yet, despite being separated from his family, face to face with the possibility of poverty, the musician becomes extremely happy. He is following his dream.

He soon plays music and teaches in a school, doing exactly what he wanted to do. And, he ends up becoming one of India's greatest musicians. Osho concludes this story with the following:

> It is not a question of his being one of the best musicians in India…what is important is that he became what he felt was his potential. And whenever you follow your potential, you always become the best. Whenever you go astray from that potential, you remain mediocre. The whole society consists of mediocre people for the simple reason that nobody is what he was destined to be—he is something else.[4]

How do you know whether you are living your true calling? It will be apparent in how you *feel*. When you live your passion you feel joy. You aren't bogged down by stress, anxiety and lethargy.

Writing, and talking to Brian or others about present-moment living I feel a sense of joy and purpose. I know it to be my true passion. I am not working a 9-5, a thought that nags at me at times, but what matters is that I feel good inside. During- and long after writing, I feel most energetic and present. Such feelings let me know I am aligned with the universe and its plans for me. Practicing the pain-body affords me no income, yet it is crucial, worthwhile and what I must do. It is important to dedicate oneself wholeheartedly to what one believes.

Albert Einstein said "Only one who devotes himself to a cause with his whole strength and soul can be a true master. For this reason mastery demands all of a person."[5] Have you mastered what you were born to do on this earth? Tolle is a master in that he fully devoted himself to living a life of presence.

He continues to master the universe's call to him by giving lectures across the globe. Indeed the words, "mastery demands all of a person," represent Tolle's journey. He gave up a prestigious Doctoral program to sit on a park bench in total presence, without knowing where his next meal would come from. He became a dropout. Yet this led to total mastery. He successfully brought his true message to the world. If he chose to get his PhD, and followed a career that no longer gave him joy, there would be no *Power of Now*. So many may have gone on sleeping, prisoners to the mind.

You may think you are nothing, that you couldn't master anything. But each one of us is meant to master, or fulfill our unique purpose.

Tolle tells us: "You are here to enable the divine purpose of the universe to unfold. That is how important you are!"[6] You are no less important than Eckhart Tolle, Albert Einstein, Harriet Tubman, Byron Katie or LeBron James. Your personal purpose is extremely important. Find it and live it, with your "whole strength."

Remember though, as any master has, you will encounter resistance from those around you. They don't want you to live your purpose because it won't make sense to them. Living your purpose may diverge significantly from what society tells you to do: get an education, work, buy a house, get married, have kids, retire, die.

It may be you sit on a park bench for two years like Tolle or lead a cause you believe in at all costs like Dr. King. Whatever it may be, live it, no matter what. No one else will be able to live the purpose designed for you. Above everything else be fully devoted to what matters most to *you*. Follow it as if your very life is at stake—because it is.

*   *   *

Time and again we face un-ideal life circumstances, and have egoic outbursts. We practice living in the Now, but still engage in arguments or indulge in useless thinking. I might cut someone off while driving, only to notice and appreciate the stillness of an oak tree at the next stop sign. Confusing right?

Average spiritual Joes are evolving. We may have outbursts, time to time. But we must let go of the guilt, and not hold it against ourselves for very long. Rather, we can learn from our low moments.

Eckhart Tolle's life is not all sunshine and rainbows. He of course still encounters challenges. However, Tolle does not create *problems* out of those challenges. He embraces the inevitable challenges of life as they occur and dissolves them, through total acceptance to what is. His lack of inner-resistance means he has no outer-resistance, or chronic, unhappy life situations.

Why is Eckhart Tolle's existence like this while we continue to struggle? His inner shift was so *great*, he had no negativity or sense-of-self left. After his radical awakening, his inside could not be more "right." His outer-reality followed suit: releasing three world-changing books, appearing on Oprah, and traveling the globe to do what he loves: talk about the Now.

Not to mention the financial abundance and world-wide popularity. Inner → Outer.

Unlike Tolle, we did not get the inside completely "right," and thus still experience pain and chaos at times on the outer layer of life. We must drop the guilt. As Tolle says, "don't fall into the error of thinking there is something wrong with you. Making yourself into a problem – the ego loves that."[7]

Just be your own witness. Catch yourself acting out your conditioning. Know it's happening while it's happening. Know at that time, the real you is not performing the conditioned behavior. Your delusional self-created problems are just that- delusional, and therefore not real. Find the humor. Next time you catch yourself slipping into a fantasy in order to avoid pain, chuckle.

Because, come on, the mind is funny! Have you ever heard a talk given by Eckhart Tolle in which there wasn't laughter? Nope. Tolle's lectures are full of humor. It's simply hilarious to see the countless manifestations of unconsciousness.

At the end of the day, if you can't laugh at yourself and the egoic behaviors you partake in, you are likely strongly identified with the ego in you. You are taking yourself, your life and your spiritual journey too seriously. So, relax, unwind and enjoy the show your ego puts on.

Stop and take a moment now. What's something funny your ego has done recently?

Brian and myself have both admitted to racing against other cars, while driving, to "beat" them, or get through green lights quicker: to win. Basically the ego sees everything as a competition. It wants to come out on top. This is humorous- driving extra-fast simply to pass the other cars on the road...we laughed at ourselves.

Expose your own conditioning by expressing it to a trusted friend. Brian and I talk every day about the unconscious mind and its manifestations. By doing so we rediscover the ego is *not* our true essence. Conversing about our destructive egoic thoughts and behaviors enables us to let go of them.

One time my pain-body became activated, I happened to be on the phone with Brian. I started getting heated, and began arguing with him. I even belittled my friend, in order to cause him pain.

Luckily Brian gently reminded me to disidentify from my negative energy. Twenty minutes later we were both laughing at my pain-body and the show it put on.

By being the witness, talking me through it and then laughing about it, Brian showed me compassion and the ultimate forgiveness. He displayed the truth: that there was no one there to forgive.

Now you may wonder, "What if I don't know anyone who reads Eckhart Tolle books?" or, "What if I don't have a friend to talk about the ego with?" That is a real possibility. Maybe your friends, family members and co-workers are not hip to their mind-identified state. You may feel spiritual loneliness. I felt that strongly, for two years, post-awakening. I remember feeling no one understood what I was going through. I even questioned if what I went through was real. But I must have surrendered to the loneliness. And soon after, I happened upon a local Eckhart Tolle Meetup group.

Don't have a "like-minded" friend? Try logging on to meetup.com and finding a Tolle group in your area. Can't find one? Start your own! Find a Present Moment-related Facebook group. Discover events or groups for meditation, yoga or other activities.

Join eckharttolletv.com. Get a dialogue going in comments sections. If you have resources and time, attend one of Eckhart Tolle's retreats or lectures, and reach out to someone there. Introduce yourself and explain that you need someone to talk to, about present-moment living. Or, if none of these work for you, give up the need to have a spiritual best friend. It's when you let go, what you 'need' miraculously arrives at your doorstep, as Tolle points out.

*

Just as inner-change produces outer-growth, outer changes also lead to inner-transformation. To get the inside "right," there are things you can do to nourish that inner-awakening, that inner-Being. We *also* must work on the outer to enhance the inner.

You may drink beer or wine each night. The alcohol makes you shift into unconsciousness, or you "fall below" the mind as Tolle describes.[8] So what is needed here? Outer change. Maybe cut alcohol out completely, and see how that affects your inner spiritual growth.

If you implement this change, you may almost immediately begin to feel a very uncomfortable sensation: the pain-body within you. By drinking alcohol each night you unconsciously numbed the old pain that is trapped in your body. But, feeling this pain is actually a huge sign of spiritual progress, and a step in the right direction.

To stop the pattern of escaping the Now through compulsive drinking, eating, smoking, thinking and doing, we must first actually *find* the pain in order to transmute it. Being aware of dysfunctional behaviors our egos produce in us, and eliminating them from our lives helps us be Present.

And, as Tolle has said, the present moment is the only place we can actually be aware of pain, in order to deal with it.

We live in a world of constant distraction. In order to fully get in touch with the present moment and thus your pain, you may need to occasionally set aside time for yourself.

One summer Brian and I planned a day of spiritual retreat. On a hot Saturday in June, I retreated in Cleveland, he in Omaha, Nebraska where he lived. I packed a notebook, pen, water bottle and some food and biked to the park.

I took no phone or electronic device. I sat on a rock and felt my inner body. I walked through a small stream, got my feet wet. I returned to nature and thus to my self. Next, I biked to an open field and lay down.

The field was covered with dandelions and robins walked about. A large willow tree stood still. The sun was beating down, giving its energy. It was colorful and clear, vibrant, almost like a scene from a movie.

During this day of personal reflection without distractions I realized within myself the reason why I <u>think</u>. Sitting by a lake where people were feeding geese, in my notebook I wrote:

What have I been running from?

The Now.

Why?

To escape thinking.

Why?

Because it hurts.

Why?

Because when I'm thinking I'm cut off from myself and I'm immersed in the collective dysfunction of the human mind. When I'm thinking or when I let myself be alone with my thoughts this is painful because insanity, ego, is painful. Yet it is important to let myself be alone with my thoughts because just underneath those thoughts is something deeper, Consciousness, who I am. So I witness the racing thoughts at first, but after a little while, the thoughts fade and I am left with my true essence, myself.

I remember how allowing my racing thoughts <u>to be</u> dissolved the thoughts. It was the first time in a long time that I had not resisted thoughts. The result was silence. Holding awareness of inner-silence nourishes Being.

Thus, a day of doing nothing can be quite helpful. This is something you can do on the outer layer of your life to enhance the inner.

Go alone. Bring a blanket and a journal and walk or bike to a nearby, quiet place in nature. Let yourself have a day free of distractions. Maybe you will discover, as I did, some inner phenomenon that will lead you back to your self.

* * *

The ego is not a menacing entity that wants the worst for us- it actually wants the best. It wants to protect us. But in doing so, it digs us deeper and deeper into a hole.

It separates us from the present moment rather than bringing us more fully into it. The ego doesn't know nothing can threaten or hurt us when we are fully in the Now. And this, Tolle says, is why the ego pushes us to constantly *escape* the Now and the pain we may discover when fully present.

Quitting alcohol or setting aside time for quiet reflection are just two examples of outer-change. Look for ways you might change your surface layer to improve your inner-life.
Now, it's likely there is an Eckhart Tolle fan out there who *recalls him saying*: "The world can only change from within." However, Tolle was not suggesting we sit back, relax and wait for our inner-selves to change completely, so that our outer lives would change for the better.

Far to the contrary. In order to evolve more fully and become more conscious, it *is* necessary to make outer changes in your life. When you have awakened to some extent, you are *able* to make true positive changes on the outer level.

For all of you who like to garden, think of how you care for your plants. Most likely, you water them, apply fertilizer, prune them and also give them your *attention*. You admire your plants. That's a natural attention that helps them grow. So begin to think of your self as a plant.

Give yourself attention in the present moment. Yes, that helps you evolve, spiritually. And take action. Just as you would fertilize and prune your flowers, you must also fertilize and prune yourself from time to time. Pay attention to the aliveness of the natural world around you.

Sit quietly among the plants you tend. Go to an Eckhart Tolle Meetup group. Participate in conversation regarding living in the Now. Take care of your body; meditate; exercise; perform tai chi; practice with the pain-body; feel the inner body; take conscious breaths.

These are all ways of taking positive steps to nourish your inner awake Being.

Pruning- getting rid of, or removing unhealthy practices, possessions or activities from our lives promotes spiritual growth. If complete spiritual awakening is the most important thing in this world, and what we want the most, deep-down, it's time to do some pruning.

PRUNE YOUR GARDEN TO ENHANCE TRUE GROWTH

For Consciousness to flourish fully, action is required, mainly, in the form of letting go. We must work to relinquish the things that prevent us from feeling pain. And, as Tolle would suggest, there first has to be an *inner* letting-go.

You can't just donate all of your possessions to charity and expect to be free of the material. For you will likely buy more objects, only to fill your house again. In order to truly "prune" destructive patterns that serve as escape routes from the Now, there has to be an authentic, inner relinquishment. In other words, you have to first *see* that your late night TV watching, Facebooking or overeating is numbing your pain and impairing your ability to be present.

More than just seeing your destructive habits, you must disidentify from them. Otherwise, guilt will creep in and you will not be able to drop such habits. Try this out.

Perhaps meditate on things you need to prune. Ask, what are my patterns for escaping the pain? Take inventory of your life and your escape-activities. This may be difficult. However, it's time to come clean with yourself and see what holds you back from enlightenment.

Once you are *aware* of your escape-routes, you must then *accept* that you have been turning off your mind and the pain, temporarily. Finally, you can prune your spiritual garden of such behaviors. The core objective in "pruning" is to lessen the strength of the ego by decreasing the activities that perpetually feed it. We must cut off the life supply of the ego.

PRUNING PROCESSES:

Smartphone or Dumbphone? You decide.

"*I fear the day that technology will surpass our human interaction. The world will have a generation of Idiots.*"[15] These words foreshadowed the current state of humanity and it is almost shocking to see how well this prediction comes true. Technology is all-pervasive and the way we use our electronic devices has become excessive.

In today's culture, it is an absolute *must* one owns a "Smartphone." With an irony of Shakespearian proportion, such devices can cause their owners to act and appear severely unintelligent, rather than smart.

The first cell phone came out on September 21st, 1983. However, the majority of people did not actively carry cell phones until the early 2000's. Now, people of all ages, cultural backgrounds and socio-economic status carry small computers with them everywhere. Please welcome a generation of idiots.

Even people who make very little money pay a high monthly bill for their Smartphone, as a basic necessity of life. And this is exactly what the ego wants. The collective ego has made cell phones a *necessity*. Most people believe they could not survive a whole 24 hours without touching their phone.

This spans the generations. Idle teenagers, Wall Street bankers, grandmothers are never far from the devices. For instance, when on a bike ride with my mother through glorious local nature reserves, we both stopped at various times to check our text messages.

The ego loves this mainstream cell phone attachment for such devices perpetually distract us from the present moment. Instead of watching the sunset as you walk down the road, you may be preoccupied Tweeting about it.

And rather than going outside and witnessing the weather, people busily check the weather conditions on an app. The way Smart phones dumb us down is by removing our focus from the present moment. Consider ways you can make yourself more intelligent and more alive in this moment in regards to your communication device:

1. Downgrade. If you have a Smartphone, you may choose to downgrade to a basic phone. Or simply cancel the "data plan" on your Smartphone and thus remove total internet access. This will remove a huge chunk of distraction. Without 24-hour access to the internet at your finger tips, and a plethora of "apps," you won't be on your phone nearly as much. If you buy a basic phone you will only use it for calling and texting and the occasional picture snapping. This will save you money, as basic phones bills are less expensive. This money could be used on outings and trips during which you may spend quality time with loved-ones, or doing something by yourself that you enjoy.

Some of you may wonder: Eckhart Tolle has an i-phone, so why can't I have one? Yes, Eckhart Tolle has admitted to having an i-phone as well as an i-pad. However, because he lives without an ego, Tolle is able to own such devices without using them to constantly escape the Now.

2. Leave Your Phone at Home. Another great way to reduce cell phone addiction is to experiment leaving your phone at home during the day. Sounds pretty extreme, but oh how liberating it can be! I remember trying this in college. Some days I left my phone at home and went to work and then to class afterwards. I felt free! Like a little kid, exploring the world without a parent. A weight was removed from my shoulders. I no longer had to attend to my communication device and could discover the world first-hand.

When I was nearing my junior year in high school my father said I could get a cell phone. I was thrilled by this. I told my family at one of our Sunday dinner gatherings. It was a scene I still vividly remember to this day. I can even recall what my family members were wearing.

When telling my family the news, I encountered much resistance. My grandparents, mother, aunt and uncle and cousins urged me not to get a cell phone. They said it would make me less connected, less present. They warned I would become attached. I would lose myself. They were very adamant about this. They were in touch with what truly matters, the simplicity of Now. Of course the teenage me didn't agree at the time. But, oh how I wish I would've listened to them and followed their advice.

Be honest with yourself: do you *truly need* to carry a cell phone with you all day? Was the part of your life in which cell phones didn't exist so *bad*? You got from here to there without a cell phone in the past, so what is stopping you now? Well, the ego of course.

The ego has created a very strong belief that you need a cell phone and must carry it with you everywhere: the grocery store, your place of work, yoga class, family gatherings, parties, and even on a walk in nature. Try leaving your phone at home just for a day. See how it feels. You can check your messages and calls in the evening. I promise, you will be more present if you try this. Warning: Your ego will not be happy with this practice.

3. Create A Cell Phone Box: Perhaps you may want to use a "Cell Phone Box." This can simply be a decorated card-board box, or a plastic container that stores your cell phones when you are with your partner or other loved ones. In this way, you are not pulled away from being present with each other. You can try this whether you are in a relationship or single. Make an effort to stash your cell phones somewhere when you are alone with someone so you are not letting cell phone use get in the way of your relationship.

Try doing this when with a close friend when out in nature or with your children during meals. Your relationships will be enhanced. You may have much more fun and feel more alive without the little computer that you carry around getting in your way.

Recently, I met up with a friend of mine at a park neither of us had ever been to. Accidentally, my friend left her phone at home. I left mine in the car. Both she and I noticed how *alive* nature was all around us. We hiked, mostly in silence among the trees and witnessed animals. We connected to our true selves. This may not have happened if either of us brought our phones, and checked our texts or took pictures. This hike became an entry to presence for me, after a long day of thinking.

*   *   *

Cell phones can be damaging to the best of relationships. It's not uncommon that couples sit side by side, all the while using their Smart phones. Even when television was the distraction, it was more intimate because a couple is engaged in the act, watching the same moving screen, able to comment on, or react together to the program.

Intimacy among humans is replaced by colder, more unfeeling technology. This is dangerous. It has implications for not only relationships among adults but for children and even pets. You may be holding your baby in one hand while using your other hand to view your bank account. I am guilty of this when it comes to my pet. Sometimes I think to go in another room to text, so my cat Bayo doesn't see me choose the phone over him.

Eckhart Tolle emphasizes the importance of being truly present when you are with people. Anyone reading this has experienced the feeling you get when someone you love chooses their phone over you.

The person you are communicating with on the phone becomes more important than those who are actually around you. At least we acknowledged the dumbing-down television introduced to our culture. Now, we deny it, calling them Smart phones.

Social Media: Are You Truly More Connected?

Another helpful pruning process is to *ease up on* or let go of social media. Not only is social media addicting but it also lacks the true connection of face-to-face interaction. In fact, such applications and websites often separate us and make us feel lonely. Anna Caltabiano of the Huffington Post illustrates this with,

Social media can create a dangerous illusion of being connected. We pay attention to numbers on Facebook and

Twitter, and often fool ourselves into thinking that we've satisfied that need to form relationships with others…people who feel the most lonely, usually have a wide and active set of "friends" on various social networks, such as Facebook.[9]

Facebook and the like present the illusion we are being social and connecting with others. However it is sadly the case most of our online activity is more in attempts to feed and enhance our egos rather than to connect with people.

For instance, posting "selfies" and pictures of the attractive outfits you wear or the places you travel, are used by the ego to build itself up. Now your social media friends know you recently went on vacation, for example, and your ego grew a little. In this way, social media reinforces your form identity. In fact, it *creates* a third identity.

There's the real you, Consciousness itself, or God. Then there's the personality (ego) "you" that you maintain in your daily life. And finally, there's the third self--the online you. This online "self" becomes real to you—each new photo you upload solidifies it.

Yet, having such a social media identity can be dangerous. Your sense-of-self is in the hands of others. If your new profile pic gets hundreds of "likes" you feel great about yourself. Yet, if no one likes your photo you might feel negative.

According to Tolle, if you know yourself as Consciousness, this polarity does not exist. Your self-esteem no longer goes up and down based on what occurs in the outer world. You stay balanced. Consciousness, your only true identity, cannot be grasped by the human mind, explains Tolle, and can neither be enhanced nor diminished. It is the essence of who you are, always have been and always will be.[10] It is untouchable.

The author of *A New Earth* explains, "You cannot lose Consciousness because it is, in essence, who you are. You can only lose something that you have, but you cannot lose something that you are."[11] Thus, if you do not know yourself as Consciousness, you will likely feel "less than" if you see a picture of your friends having fun and they forgot to invite you. You may feel superior to someone else, based on their posts. In either case, this strengthens your form identity. You are not better or worse than anyone else, for we are all the same Consciousness.

Perhaps it's time to prune your social media addiction if you have one. If you do this you will have less overall mind activity. You will have one less "self" to maintain. Nature will re-enter your daily existence.

Psychotropic Medications: Form of Healing or Temporary Escape?

Eckhart Tolle describes how many people, because of their pain-body, suffer from almost constant emotional pain. These people are innocently led to believe by either surfing the web, or being told by loved ones or doctors, they have an imbalance of chemicals in their brain leading to feelings such as intense sadness and unbearable anxiety. They are told they have a disorder, that there is something *wrong* with them. Such individuals rightfully seek out professional help in attempts to somehow cope with their "imbalance."

There is nothing wrong with wanting to alleviate immense pain or in requesting help. However, most professionals, not knowing how to heal a person's pain on an inner level are too quick to diagnose someone with a mental disorder and write them a prescription.

Medications such as anti-anxiety pills and anti-depressants do a great job in reducing symptoms. In fact, over time, you may believe your daily medication has healed you of depression for good. However, what happens when you eventually stop taking your once a day pill?

The depressive or fearful feelings reappear. In fact, many people, even after properly weaning themselves off a medication desire to commit suicide. Why does this happen? Because the pill they were taking once a day continuously numbed the pain within them. Under the surface, the pain lay dormant.

In this way, psychotropic medications are not unlike other pain-escaping addictions such as illegal drug use. Anti-depressants and the like provide you with the illusion you are healed from your emotional pain.

But, as Tolle would ask, do you want to live with the illusion that you are free? Does that really heal you? Of course it doesn't.

I am going out on a limb to state that illnesses such as Major Depressive Disorder, Anxiety Disorder, Bi-Polar Disorder and the myriad of mental disorders are quite simply pronounced pain-body afflictions. In other words, a person who has so-called "Clinical Depression" is suffering from an accumulation of pain, which formed into a very heavy pain-body.

Tolle has illustrated this phenomenon in his works. The pain-body is not unrelated to brain chemistry. A depressed, anxious, or manic individual's pain-body is dense. But as Tolle would point out, what would you expect within a society that has killed 150 million plus of its own species in the last 100-150 years?[12]

The fact our very existence makes us necessarily complicit in destroying our own ecosystems is a sad, heavy thing on its own. Now add in past hurts and harms-done to us, or that we committed. The sadness, the pain gets deeper and deeper. Such pain can take over.

A person with a less heavy pain-body experiences emotional pain less frequently, Tolle says, but one with a very dense pain-body experiences the pain continuously and is thus diagnosed with a mental disorder. Tolle says it's as if the pain-body is living through them and influencing all of their actions, behaviors and thoughts, constantly. And a doctor instructs that person to take an anti-depressant to fix the problem.

But, as anyone reading this book, and anyone who has experienced taking such medications and *stopped* taking them knows, the pain-body cannot be transmuted by taking a pill. In fact, it can only be diverted temporarily. Psychotropic drug use is truly akin to an alcoholic drinking each day to numb their pain. It doesn't work and ends up causing the pain to grow.

You may be wondering how I know this information to be true. I do not have the initials M.D. after my name. I believe it to be true because I experienced it personally, and then read Eckhart Tolle's works, which only confirmed my faith. I now offer my own personal experience with anti-anxiety medications and anti-depressants:

At age 19 I was very suicidal. I didn't know it then, but I now know that I was living with an extremely heavy pain-body.

I had visions of being hit by a car and sometimes I would stand on the sidewalk quite close to the street and watch the cars speeding by. I would feel a rush inside and a pull to jump out in front of the cars.

It got to the point where I was laying down on the ground sobbing, expressing verbally that I just wanted to die. My parents, not knowing that I was suffering from the pain-body, took me to see a doctor, who within minutes wrote me prescriptions for anti-depressant and anti-anxiety medications.

Pretty soon I no longer felt the urge to die. In fact, I felt better quite quickly. I then began training for a marathon, entered into a new relationship and was getting all A's in my first year of college.

I was eating healthy again and exercising a lot, and I moved out of my mother's house. I was independent, and on the surface level was pretty happy.

When I was 20 I read A New Earth *as well as* The Power of Now *for the second time. Yet it was this time around that I actually had an awakening when reading the books. Soon, I was totally devoted to Eckhart Tolle's teachings. I lived in a state of contentment, and joy for over two years.*

At 21, under a doctor's instruction, I removed myself from the anti-anxiety medication. For I no longer experienced intense anxiety. By the time I turned 23, I had a desire to stop taking the anti-depressant as well. With the help of a doctor, I got off that medication. I believed that in order to fully feel my inner body and practice Eckhart's teachings I must quit the medication.

Soon after stopping the medication that I was taking once a day for 4 years, the pain-body re-emerged in me. It took me over and again, I found myself wanting to either kill myself or for an asteroid to wipe out the earth. I was back at square one. "What was the point?" I asked my best friend.

Thankfully, I had read Tolle's works within that 4-year time span and had that initial, irreversible awakening. Thus, this time around in coping with the pain, instead of popping a daily pill, I knew it was time to practice with the pain-body once a day instead.

I found the practice became more authentic and more meaningful as well as healing for me, now that my brain was no longer being numbed by chemicals in the form of medications.

I could finally sit with the pain, actually feel it shaking within me and hold it for at least a minute or two and allow it to be. I knew deep down my individual pain was extremely heavy--heavier than most.

This same heaviness was why I wanted to die when I was 19. I wanted to be free of such pain. Tolle has taught me that the only way to be free of it is to love it: to embrace it, give it a metaphorical hug within, and simply notice it.
Today, after a lot of pain-body practice I am no longer depressed or suffer from anxiety. Medications are no longer necessary.

Yes, I still have a pain-body, but it is a lot lighter. Am I fully awake yet? No. Because the pain within me comes up. Do I faithfully sit with it every single time?

No, I still resist doing so. But I do sit with it and work on transmuting it often, and that is what has made all the difference.

It is clear to see that if you are depressed or chronically anxious, you may be *able* to dissolve some of the heavy pain, little by little, by practicing Tolle's pain-body technique.

Under medical advice and with a master plan your doctor provides, you may be able to change your chemistry for the better by pruning a drug from your life.

Whether you stay on a drug or not, it is vital to live consciously and become fully awake. Medications may prevent you from fully facing your pain-body to prune it. Talk to your physician about this.

Embracing your pain is the key to the "kingdom of heaven." In fact, if Jesus were alive today, he would probably say something along the lines of "he who takes an anti-depressant each day is not fit for the kingdom of heaven."

Facing your pain here and now automatically brings you to the present moment, or the kingdom of heaven. Walk *through* the doorway of pain, rather than *around* it, and enter the Now. Go through the gates of hell and thus enter heaven.

* **I am not offering you medical advice.** If you are on a psychotropic medication, desire to be, or want to stop taking a medication, talk to your doctor first.

Overeating: What are you Avoiding?

Because food is necessary for survival, easily accessible, an expression of love that can also be inexpensive, and legal for anyone to buy, many people use overeating as an escape from the Now. In fact it is common for individuals to use food in the same way an infant would use a pacifier to soothe itself: people eat to calm themselves of strong emotions.

This is known as stress-eating. What has become increasingly common is binge-eating, or eating an enormous quantity of food in one sitting.

Individuals who binge-eat usually do so in isolation, in order to avoid the shame of others. The quantity of food consumed usually correlates with the amount of pain the individual is attempting to escape from. Moreover the speed at which the food is consumed is another indicator of heavy emotional pain.

People who eat to numb their pain often devour food quickly without even really tasting it. Type of food is also important. Individuals who use food as a drug don't typically overeat on carrots or Swiss chard.

Rather, high calorie options are consumed such as refined carbohydrates, greasy fried foods and what seems to be most common: sugar. Why? Because such foods release high levels of dopamine, and that translates into us feeling pleasure. And the ego, in attempts to protect us from feeling pain, will literally force us to engage in behaviors that cause us to experience pleasure.

This is usually an unconscious process. Eckhart Tolle brought this overeating issue to light in his books. Yet even after reading about the process, many still struggle with the issue today. Why? Only because there is still pain there, and the individual has not yet pruned his or her *emotional* garden.

If you don't know there is pain in you, you will continue to act out unhealthy escape patterns. Once the habit is acknowledged and pruned, and the pain transmuted, there will not be an ego-induced urge to eat more than what the body needs.

Overeating is widespread. Humanity has become increasingly insane. In fact, in America, over one third of adults are obese and 1 in 5 are overweight.[13] Being overweight or obese negatively impacts individual's lives in considerable ways. Low self-esteem along with social isolation and a myriad of health problems are often the case.

Those who are of a *healthy* weight also use food to avoid pain. Even overeating small amounts has negative effects. Because either way, you are using food to consistently block pain from coming up. Just as drinking a little each night to numb the pain is detrimental to your spiritual progress, even though you are not an alcoholic.

Below are a couple tips for anyone who is in the throws of a food addiction. But remember: no matter how often you overeat, or how many diets you go on, you will not be freed of this issue unless and until you completely deal with your pain-body 100%.

1. *Reach out:* This is probably the hardest thing one can do when addicted to food. Overeating is one of the most shameful addictions. Many people view overeating as a weakness, not an addiction and thus shame the food-addicted person rather than

offer help. Also, many people are very embarrassed of binge-eating.

It seems that it is actually more socially acceptable for an individual to be alcoholic or a smoker than a food-addict. And thus, many people do not ask for help when struggling with this problem.

However, calling a friend on the phone may be enough to pull you out of a heavy urge to binge. Support from either a trusted friend, partner or family member is key here.

Moreover, if your overeating habit is exceedingly threatening to your health, perhaps see a counselor. Talk therapy may expose your overeating habit and weaken it.

Whatever you do, know you are not alone. Trust that your overeating habit is *not* who you are. It is a temporary mind pattern that is used as an escape-route from feeling painful emotions.

2. *Reduce or cut out Sugar*: According to Kris Gunnars, of Authority Nutrition, "Sugar….due to its powerful effect on the reward centers of the brain, functions similarly to drugs of abuse like cocaine and nicotine."[14]

This means anyone who uses food as an escape should lower their sugar intake. This can be done by cutting out drinks containing added sugars as well as reducing intake of high-sugar cereals, snacks and desserts. Because it is so addictive, it can be hard to kick an overeating habit at all, if excess sugar is present in the diet.

Overall, it is important to be aware of why you are overeating or binging. It is clearly because you want to avoid something. Otherwise you would not actively engage in behaviors that are destructive towards the health of your body.

*

It is not just overeating or binging on food that is used to perpetually escape pain. Starving yourself, chronic dieting or having an extreme focus on what you eat is the flip side of the same coin.

Yes, under-eating, and obsessing over food, calories and nutrition, just like overeating, is used to avoid pain. Instead of letting go of control and facing emotional pain, such individuals control their *food consumption* to avoid being present.

Focusing on grams of fat or sugar in food products for instance, or obsessively measuring what you eat, talking about how you don't eat a certain food group, constantly thinking about food, is a form of escape.

You place your full attention on something that is necessary for survival: food. Yet this attention and control is unbalanced. It's too much. It's like a drug, just as binge-eaters use food to numb pain.

If you have an addiction to dieting or obsessing about food it might be time to prune yourself of this unhealthy attachment. Yes, be mindful of what you eat, of course. But don't let *food* take over your entire life. Have your full attention in the Now. Let go of control.

Pain will arise, but have the courage to face it rather than completely filling up your space with facts or rituals. There is such a thing as too healthy. Be yourself.

Many have an unhealthy relationship to food in attempts to stay or become thin, or to look a certain way. This is escape. Rather than being yourself in the present, you are constantly focused on achieving some future state of thinness or physical attractiveness.

You are never content with what is. Always searching for completion in the future by becoming more. In this case, the "more" is becoming more physically attractive. This is a total focus on what you look like and has nothing to do with who you *are*.

This can be a very difficult habit to prune because our society is so focused on outer appearance. However, it is a worthwhile and very liberating pattern to *notice* and then release.

In fact, the more *present* you are and fully *content* with what is, the more beautiful you look physically. The joy you feel within shines through your outer appearance, making you beautiful in a way that no make up or body type could measure up to.

*   *   *

As far as Pruning Practices, or steps you can take to reduce the strong pull of addictive, ego-driven behaviors, the focus has been on: Smartphone use, social media, psychotropic medication use and overeating.

There are many more practices you can initiate to reduce mind activity in your daily life. Think about what really sucks you out of being present in this moment. Is it your phone or your Facebook page? Then try implementing some of the pointers above.

However, it could be something totally different, such as habitual television watching or gambling. If that is the case, be creative and think of something *concrete* you can do *right now* to reduce the strong, addictive force of the ego and its hold on you.

The key is focusing on small actions you can take.

I am not asking you to be perfect and to live at a Buddhist monastery for the rest of your life. That is not realistic for most people. What is more important is to take steps to cut down mind activity and thereby increase aliveness in your daily existence.

Distractions are abundant and easily accessible. Thus, it is important to do your part to make sure the things of this world do not take up 100% of your attention at all times. These are individual actions you can take on your own.

Next we turn to part two of this book, which focuses on communal actions we can take to access the New Earth here and now.

JOINT EFFORTS TOWARDS TOTAL AWAKENED LIVING

A CALL TO COMMUNITY: THE NEW EARTH

The final chapter of this book is the most important. The previous chapters explored common experiences along the path of awakening.

We are now conscious of our ego's effect on us, as we shift in and out of the present moment. This common journey and shared experience manifests in us an irrevocable bond of trust, and oneness.

*We can see more clearly that at times, **all** of us semi-awakened individuals get swept up by the mind and pain-body every now and then.*

Recognizing the ego within us and sharing it with others is power. Our shared experience is the basis of true Community.

The next evolution of humanity is what we do with the shared experience. As our Community develops, we will cease to shift in and out of Consciousness.

Yes, the human ego is pervasive. However, the collective ego will shrink in power as our Community grows in strength. What will take over is trust in life and authentic, joyous living, as the kingdom of heaven, or the New Earth takes shape.

CHAPTER FIVE
THE COMMUNITY OF PRESENCE

You may feel you do not fit in this world. Perhaps this is a subtle feeling you experienced throughout your life, even as a child.

The fact is, if you are reading this, you don't belong. You don't fit in. Even if you are a member of social clubs, teams and organizations, it is likely that no matter *what* you identify with, you end up feeling like an outcast in some way. Particularly having awakened, you may feel less connected to many people around you, as Eckhart Tolle mentioned in *A New Earth*.[1]

Do not be down on yourself for not belonging, for the ego will only use that to strengthen itself. The ego feeds on any type of resistance, no matter what form it takes, as Tolle points out. Instead, try to look at this phenomenon in a positive light. According to Marcus Aurelius, "The object of life is not to be on the side of the majority, but to escape finding oneself in the ranks of the insane."[2]

Be thankful you don't fit into this world. If you fit, you would be another walking ego.

Although I didn't understand why, throughout my life I felt like an outcast, even on teams, at jobs or within organizations. Thankfully I formed authentic friendships with others, who like me did not fit the cookie cutters. The bonds I developed with outsiders enabled me to experience joy, love and true connection.

However, deep down, I still felt something was wrong with me. Even though I managed to meet plenty who also did not fit in, I didn't understand why we didn't fit, and this made me suffer.

Sometimes I resisted being an outcast. This caused me pain. However, I have since accepted it. I no longer expect myself to fit, and cannot be disappointed. It feels so good to be free of that burden. I was able to drop the resistance once I realized Consciousness doesn't *want* me to totally fit in- and will never *let me*. For if I fit in, I wouldn't have a need or even the desire to become fully awake. The reason YOU don't fit in is because you are needed to help build the New Earth that Tolle speaks of.

Consciousness is utilizing you to help pave the way towards the next evolution of humanity. That is why it is crucial that you are unable to fit in. It is as though Consciousness continuously reminds you that you were never meant to settle down in this world, that you instead exist to work towards the creation of a new one.

Tolle uses the metaphor of the fish and evolution. Just as long, long ago some fish leapt out of the sea, grew legs and became human beings, you are in the process of leaping out of the *mind* and will evolve into a new, awakened form of human. In fact, this process is already happening in you. You have to do this, for the good of humanity and of the Earth. If you fight this drive within, you experience pain.

Imagine if those initial fish fought the urge to leap out of the sea. What if they tried to fit in with all of the other fish who were content living under water? Where would we be?

Post-awakening, you live differently. Others will likely criticize you for this, as Einstein's words point to: "Great spirits have always encountered violent opposition from mediocre minds."[3]

Most people, under the control of the ego, live at the level of mind. Mind is unable to recognize spirit. This is why the majority may "violently oppose" you as Einstein said—for you live from Consciousness and those who live from ego do not understand you. Because they don't understand you, they fear you. They may hate you.

"If you belonged to the world, it would love you as its own. As it is, you do not belong to the world, but I have chosen you out of the world. That is why the world hates you."[4] Here, when Jesus says, "I have chosen you," he is not literally talking about himself but rather Consciousness, the sacred, the Tao, the One.

Consciousness has chosen you to build the New Earth. Focus on that. You build your spirit, and this simultaneously strengthens the builders around you. The foundation is one foundation. It will only get you off-track if you bother working to fit in with those who will inevitably oppose you.

* * *

Tolle depicted the phenomenon of the "frequency holders" in *A New Earth*. Such people, according to Tolle, feel almost unable to live within our human society and find living a "normal" life focused mainly on career and marriage quite challenging.

Instead, they live as they are compelled inwardly to do. Theirs is a simple life, for they live in accord with the frequency of Presence in their day-to-day, as Tolle explains. If you are a so-called frequency holder, or if you find living in this world difficult for whatever reason, I believe the development of a wide-spread global spiritual community will be quite comforting for you.

Such a community will provide a safe space for you to connect on an authentic level with other awakening individuals in an environment of pure presence. This community will offer you a respite from the mad world around you. This is what this chapter is all about.

*

During high school, I remember wishing I lived in a world in which there were only animals, elderly people and children. I no longer desire this of course, and to many, such a wish would seem insane.

But in a way, it makes sense.

Animals are ego-less beings covered in fur, scales, fins. Children are not yet filled with heavy mind conditioning and pain-body. It is refreshing to be in the presence of animals and children. You feel at ease, and often find yourself becoming free of mind in their presence, as Tolle points out.

Elderly people can be pleasant to be around for similar reasons. They are less likely to be competing or racing. They no longer tend to focus on what their future will look like. Some older people were able to let go of the heavy burden of mind they carried around during their adult lives.

They have lived for so many years, they know the things young people worry about are not *that* important.

Before my late grandfather passed he seemed to be quite awake to his true essence. When people would comment on things or question him, he would often respond with "I dunno," or simply, "whatever."

My grandfather's "whatever," which he said with a slight smile, reminded me that life is temporary and not something to take too seriously.

It is good to take things seriously to some extent, so things are as great as we can make them. But mostly, it is best to see the way things are and feel okay about them. We need to do what we can, but have peace in our hearts and minds, rather than the mind's constant restlessness.

My teenage wish to live in a world of ego-less or slightly ego-less beings came from a common desire to live in a world in which the ego did not *dominate people's lives*. I wanted so badly to be surrounded by people who were also on the awakening journey. But because that was not yet the case, I felt lonely and out of place in the world, as I had for the majority of my life.

It can be a lonely, confusing existence for many people who are on the path of awakening because the natural, human desire to fit in is so strong in people. It is deeply rooted in our psyches. When we do feel out of place this threatens the ego tremendously.

The ego wants nothing more than to fit in, build itself up, and even stand out. But for those who have become awakened, it is almost impossible to be understood by others and fit in. Unless, they are surrounded by other awakened people.

Brian, myself and so many other "average spiritual Joes" don't want to live the rest of our existences in a world in which we continuously come up against the workings of the egos of the people around us. We no longer want to get sucked into that ego drama ourselves.

We want to actually *witness* and live in the New Earth that Tolle talked about, that the Bible foreshadowed. We desire nothing more than to live in a world in which the majority-not minority- of people are awakened.

Because let's get real here. Although *many* people on the Earth *are* becoming awakened, this is not the "New Earth" that Tolle pointed to. Far from it.

The "New Earth" is comprised of two realities: an individual's inner reality, and that of the world as a whole. A person may be awakened and experience joy and aliveness on a consistent basis. And that is great. That is the foundation of what Tolle pointed to when he spoke of the New Earth. It is a way of living.

However, the outer reality is not yet that of the New Earth. Shootings, political warfare, terrorism, starvation and emotional and physical violence within the home are clear indicators that as a human race, we are still living on the Old Earth.

So it is time that people who are devoted to awakening take *active* steps to bring the New Earth about. According to Tolle, it simply takes *enough people waking up* from their conditioning for it to arise.

* * *

The loneliness I spoke of above is not something I feel anymore. I know myself primarily as Being and not just as a "little me." Meeting individuals strongly-rooted in presence has been a gift, and the boost I need. And as I go on I meet more. I am drawn towards them, and they to me.

Brian and I talk every day. We converse about our own egoic patterns and the crazy ego-run world we live in. We consider each other "pain-body partners" and "spiritual sponsors." When the pain-body arises, we share this with each other. This stimulates that transmutation of pain Tolle says is so important.

The discussions I have with Brian are always refreshing. When I speak to him and discover he is having the same experiences I am, I feel connected to another human being. Primarily, my Consciousness feels one with that of Brian's. For it is all the same Consciousness manifesting in a multitude of forms, as Tolle has explained. In that state of communion the ego loses its power and truly does not seem to exist.

Brian and I are just two individuals, but we make our own spiritual community. Without him and the ability to share my experiences with him, I do not know where I would be. Thus, he and I are answering the call to assist in the manifestation of a widespread community of individuals around the world. No one will feel lonely or out of place anymore, and eventually this community will collectively manifest Consciousness on a scale not seen before in the history of the human species.

Global presence power will take over and we will see the New Earth with our very own eyes. The New Earth wants to come into existence. To build the New Earth and live in it, it is necessary for awakened people to join together to become and to work towards enlightened living.

The universe has passed the baton from one magnificent individual to the rest us. Now comes the next crucial step in global awakening. Jesus said,

> *For where two or three are gathered together in My name, I am there in the midst of them.*[5]

When you are with other awakening individuals, you can feel Presence more strongly.

An example of this is when Brian, who was living in Nebraska at the time, came to Cleveland, Ohio where I live to visit. During his December 2014 visit, we spent a day together. By evening we found ourselves eating frozen yogurt at a nearby café.

There were about five other people there. Brian and I began talking about presence in daily life. Then, we stopped talking and sat in silence. We observed the café, each other and the people around us. All at once Brian and I experienced the strongest satori that we have ever felt. I remember my legs and arms radiated with presence.

I felt my inner body so strongly it was overwhelming. My senses were impacted as well. The colors of everything around me became intense and I felt a peace so strong I could barely speak. It simply felt so right to be exactly where I was. I felt wide awake, no longer totally absorbed in the dream of form.

I could tell Brian was feeling the same way and he verbally confirmed so. About 20 minutes went by, which felt like an eternity, and the café was closing. Brian and I got into the car and he drove me home. The whole time we were driving we both still felt that peace.

It was good to be alive.

I labeled the above experience as satori because to me and to Brian it was more than simply being present. It was a total-body experience of utter Consciousness; it was a recognizable flash of enlightenment itself. The heavy layer of unconscious mind was removed. Brian and I still talk about that time at the café.

And, I bring it up here because it illustrates Jesus' words. Two individuals gathered in presence and Consciousness. God was there, for we had abandoned ourselves, which left just the soul. Moreover, the experience represents what a community of awakening humans can bring about: heightened aliveness, satori, peace, enlightenment.

During that time period in the café Brian and I were living in the New Earth. We both experienced directly what that felt like. And it could not have felt better. Although we were simply eating frozen yogurt and observing those around us, we experienced directly the kingdom of heaven, the "Pure Land."

We can take those moments from our lives and carry them over into the next moment.

Breathing in, taking some time to re-feel what we felt before bed, or when stepping out of bed to greet the day, we remind ourselves it is possible to feel that anytime we want to. To share a moment with another on the path tells us we are not alone! It happens to be we fit in with those who are awake, rather than the sleeping majority. We *truly* fit in only when the human part of us dissolves and we are in touch with our God-essence.

This book is a call for that type of community to form so that all people feel such presence on a daily basis. Brian and I didn't have to *do anything* to access that realm. We simply entered the Now, *together*. And the results were mind-blowing. The experience reminded us of Eckhart Tolle's words in *The Power of Now*:

> If you are fortunate enough to find someone who is intensely conscious, if you can be with them and join them in the state of presence, that can be helpful and will accelerate things. In this way your own light will quickly grow stronger. When a log that has only just started to burn is placed next to one that is burning fiercely, and after a while they separate again, the first log will be burning with much greater intensity. After all, it is the same fire.[6]

Brian and I are only two "logs" out of millions. If we simply sat in a café and generated enough presence power to feel our inner bodies fiercely and experience a state of unforgettable bliss, imagine what the world would be like if multitudes of people came together in a state of Presence to discuss Consciousness and to live fully in the Now.

There is nothing special about Brian or myself. We are simply two average spiritual Joes who are on the awakening journey. In fact, the very same day, before meeting up with Brian, I was caught in the pain-body for two hours. Similarly, my friend shared he was trapped in racing mind activity before our visit that December day.

This points to the importance of community and the meaning behind Jesus' words, highlighted by Tolle in *A New Earth*: "I can of my own self do nothing."[7] As individuals on the awakening journey we experience getting trapped in continuous thinking and the negative emotions of the pain-body.

However, if we come together and share our common journey in a state of Oneness, miracles can happen.

Connect with one who is awakening. Surround yourself with those who want to live consciously. Begin with one kindred spirit, but be always seeking more. Find a community, or make one. Consciousness can more thoroughly work through humans if they come together in presence.

If we could do it on our own then we would already be fully awake. Yet we are not. As Tolle would say, look at your actions and thought processes or simply turn on the nightly news and you will see the current state of humanity and the dilemma of mind-dominated living. The Universe wants there to be a community of presence on this world.

*

There is a multitude of spiritual resources and practices, but those things have been around for a long, long time, and where is the New Earth?

Is perfecting the Triangle Pose really going to cause a widespread awakening of the entire globe? Is learning how to perform Reiki going to change your existence, totally free you of mind-possession and help you feel truly connected with the people around you?

The answer of course is no. At this time, what is *more important* than such individual practices is the formation of *widespread spiritual community*. And- each of us must work to fully dissolve our pain-body. As we dissolve our pain-bodies we interact with others, and these interactions wear away at all of our pain-bodies. In order for people to **fully** transmute their pain-body what is needed most *is* a spiritual community.

If the universe wanted you and the millions of other people currently walking the spiritual path to awaken all at once and be instantly free of all past pain and mind conditioning, that would've happened. But as you know, this is not the case. Consciousness would find joy in witnessing its creation, humans, coming together build the New Earth. Life is a dance, as Tolle says, and the creation of a spiritual community is one of the universe's many beautiful "moves."

Many people had an awakening, yet reached their death without enlightenment. They never got to see a planet in which people live fully in the present moment. So many people walk with one foot in and one foot out of the spiritual realm. People are tired of knowing what it means to be truly present, yet act out their compulsive, egoic conditioning. Take this Bible quote:

> Enter through the narrow gate. For wide is the gate and broad is the road that leads to destruction, and many enter through it. But small is the gate and narrow the road that leads to life, and only a few find it.[8]

According to Jesus, "only a few find it." And he was one of them. Only a few know what it is like to live their lives *continuously* awake in the Now.

Nearly everyone lives in a state of destruction. That is the ego's main symptom: destruction. The ego, with its pain-body causes even awakened individuals to destruct and obstruct things.

When you blow up on your partner or argue with a friend, that is destructive. When you eat a whole bag of chips to avoid the pain you feel inside, that is destructive to your body. And when you constantly judge or resist this moment and the people around you that only leads to destructive thoughts, emotions and actions. And--as within, so without. We live in a world in which people use guns, bombs and other weapons to literally destruct people and things around them.

A spiritual Community will make the narrow gate wider, so that millions and eventually billions of people walk through it. In so doing, the "wide gate that leads to destruction" will become smaller until it is barely noticeable anymore, and eventually there will no longer be a need to destruct things.

* * *

Tolle laid the foundation for us. His teaching on the pain-body is invaluable. But it is only the foundation. In this way it is incomplete. We must add to the foundation. What's needed now is *coming together in community* to dissolve the pain-body.

One spring evening I sensed a bit of negative energy within. Yet, I didn't have the strength or willingness to sit with it. I had the night off work so I decided to spend time with my girlfriend, Shanice. When I arrived at her house we decided to go to a nearby park. I admitted I had been feeling some pain for hours, but resisted facing it. When we got to the park, I spontaneously requested she sit with me while I face my pain.

She was up for it.

It was dark and very quiet that night at the empty park. Shanice and I sat on a picnic table in silence. She sat quite close to me and held my hand. I felt her presence- she was not distracted by anything. She was focused solely on being there. "I'm gonna go into the pain now," I mumbled. I went into my body, and boom! Instantly, I felt a tremendous surge of pain. My whole body was radiating with old, blocked negative energy.

I started to cry almost immediately. But even while sobbing I held the pain with my conscious attention. It was like nothing I had ever experienced. The pain was *fully* there and it was so *easy* for me to feel it. It was overwhelming but inviting at the same time. There was no other choice but to feel it.

Shanice was gracefully there for me the whole time I held my pain. She didn't comment or pull away. After feeling my pain so strongly for minutes, I thanked her. I realized right away that it was *her presence*, which enabled me to so easily find and transmute some of my pain-body that night. It was an ah-ha moment for me. I discovered first-hand, being together in presence when dealing with the pain-body provides the quickest, easiest way of transmuting it. It further confirmed how necessary community is.

At the café with Brian I experienced satori- the ecstasy of being fully awake in the moment. In the park with Shanice I experienced the closest contact with the pain-body that I ever had. Both were invaluable experiences that led to an effortless entry to Being. And both have one thing in common: Community.

COMMUNITY OF PRESENCE MEETINGS

I of my own self can do nothing.[7]

John 5:30

Alcoholism, like compulsive thinking, is a destructive addiction. Yet, In 1935, in Akron, Ohio, Bill Wilson and Dr. Bob Smith came together to form a global community of individuals devoted to becoming and living sober: Alcoholics Anonymous. AA has changed the destructive problem of alcoholism. AA, a widespread community of like-minded people, positively impacts the lives of millions, transforming them from destructive to sober.

AA helps people walk through the gate of sobriety. Whereas sobriety used to be a narrow gate, one almost impossible to walk through for alcoholics, now it is wide, because of the community. Many would call AA a lifesaver.

Every day of the year, in practically every city around the world there are AA meetings that provide refuge and support in becoming sober. And of course, there are 12-step communities for a myriad of addictions such as drug abuse, overeating, anger problems and gambling.

But what about the disease of unconsciousness, of mind-dominated living? Isn't that just as compulsive, destructive and overwhelming as having another addiction, such as alcoholism or food addiction?

The answer is yes, for unconsciousness causes suffering. It forces people to be destructive in order to avoid pain at any cost. Unconsciousness drives people to drink too much alcohol, gamble or overeat in the first place!

Awakened people should be able to join a Community of Presence, just as alcoholics are able to take part in AA. There can be community meetings, all day, every day, in every city or town just for Conscious people building the New Earth. Meetings mirroring the ones for twelve-step programs will nourish awakening in people, and speed up the enlightenment process.

*   *   *

What might happen at Community of Presence meetings? Well, no one could predict the amazing things that may occur when people come together in the Now. However, I imagine individuals freely expressing the ups and downs of their spiritual journeys.

Being open and honest with other like-minded people creates a strong sense of community and also personal strength. An individual at a community meeting being able to express that they are stuck in thinking would help that person to step out of the mind and enable others in the room to do the same.

Sharing is exposing the ego directly, and thus can be a form of ego death. The ego has a greater chance of getting you to identify with it if you keep it bottled up. This is why talk-therapy can be beneficial to people.

I've had therapy to get through rough times. It could only do so much for me. It was like stopping the bleed on a cut. It provided symptom relief but didn't go deep enough. No therapist I've been to was well-read in Tolle. I remember wanting whichever therapist to intentionally sit with me in presence, and be the space for my pain-body. For that was what I truly needed at the time. That is what we can do for each other at meetings.

I don't need to wait for a therapist who is knowledgeable of Tolle's pain-body practice. My friend Brian and my girlfriend Shanice provide their presence, free of charge, anytime and this enables me to face my pain fully. This is my personal community. Imagine a global one!

We need to come together, and provide the type of support that can change the world and remove the need for therapy in the first place.

Joining together to talk about the difficulties of egoic conditioning and pain not only creates a sense of compassion but also a feeling of not being alone on the journey. I remember after first awakening, I tried talking about being in the present moment with friends and family members, yet they didn't seem all that interested. Thus I felt alienated in a world that didn't understand the importance of "being still and knowing."

Luckily, I discovered and joined a local Eckhart Tolle Meet-up Group in Beachwood, Ohio. The Meetups were great because I connected with people who were going through the same thing I was. This not only more deeply confirmed within me the truth of present moment living, but also strengthened my presence power. It felt so good to spend an hour and a half with people who were devoted to the only thing that truly matters.

A couple years later I met Brian at one of the Meet-up sessions. We traded contact info and soon became not only best friends but each others' spiritual teacher and simultaneous student.

The Eckhart Tolle Meet-up Group is invaluable, yet the meetings are generally once a month and sometimes, one of the monthly meetings get canceled for one reason or another. There must be meetings accessible to all, every day.

The possibility to attend meet-ups or Community of Presence meetings on a daily basis would aid so many who walk the path. The journey of awakening can be littered with time periods of doubt and confusion. Many people who are affiliated with AA firmly believe that alcoholic individuals cannot recover without AA or some other support system, outside of themselves. The same applies to all of us "average spiritual Joes."

We need the support of one another to encourage present moment living within ourselves, share our shortcomings and be the space for each other's pain. We need a Community of Presence.

*

The Community of Presence would not be a religion. No one would worship Eckhart Tolle or Kim Eng as being God. Instead the community would be a *space* of stillness and presence where journeyers find respite- shelter from their busy, hectic lives. It would be a time to share freely with others, to develop friendships, to reach out, ask questions or to simply observe in silence.

During the meetings there will be much laughter because the recognition of "Oh I do that too!" can be funny, and also very freeing. Further, true connections will be formed at such gatherings. Phone lists, pot lucks and picnics can be arranged.

People at such meetings would not come *only* from the surface layer. Individuals would not simply be trying to impress others to enhance their ego. Instead, they would be coming from pure presence, the inner realm, the deeper place. Only from that place can true connection arise, as Tolle teaches.

Thus the Community of Presence would destruct loneliness while building true friendships on this planet.

*

I remember when sitting in silence with others during an Eckhart Tolle Meet-up I attended, I felt so intensely alive, without *trying* to. The group leader, Larry, even commented on how strong the group's energy felt. Because the group as a whole generated much presence, individually it was so easy to feel the inner body.

At Community of Presence meetings this same phenomenon will take place. The presence generated will be palpable. Individuals will still be able to feel that aliveness within them when they arrive home, which in turn will cause a chain reaction of awakening. In truth, it will change the world as we know it.

A Suggested Blueprint for the Community of Presence

Website

Today everything is online. Therefore, it will be necessary for the Community of Presence to have a main website listing local meeting times and locations, as well as nearby events or retreats. Free articles and videos will be accessible on the site, as well as schedules for the meetings, searchable by zip code. Books and other media will be sold to pay for the spaces we use for meetings. Further, many who for some reason or another would be unable to physically attend meetings could read excerpts, passages, essays and personal narratives by members of the Community of Presence. There may even be online meetings. Individuals can use the Community website to figure out where new meetings are needed, in the city they live.

Initially, this could be done through Meetup.com. Brian and I recently set up a "Community of Presence" meet-up group in Cleveland.

Cost

Finances may prevent individuals from attending certain classes or workshops. Many people who are on the awakening journey do not have access to a thousand dollars to attend a retreat, for example.

We may want to treat ourselves to a relaxing massage to reduce stress or attend a lecture but have limited funds to do so. Thus, money should *not* impair one's ability to be part of the Community of Presence. In order for the Community to be accessible to *all*, I propose it be free of charge, as AA is, with only suggested donations of a dollar or two to pay the church or other facility providing the Community the space for meetings.

Pain-Body Circles

I propose there be pain-body circles at Community of Presence meetings, where people can sit in silence, and feel their pain-bodies *together*.

It may begin with a short meditation to bring about stillness and then a guided inner-exploration to find blocked pain within. Then, individuals within the circle could hold their personal pain in silent Presence. This would be a form of collective transmutation of the pain-body.

Participating in pain-body circles will afford people to more easily access and actually hold their pain, when part of a group, rather than doing so alone. Fifteen to twenty-minute pain-body circles could take place at some point during each meeting. Or, pain-body circles could be offered once a week as a separate meeting of their own, and take up a full meeting's duration. The important thing is making sure to hold one's pain during the circle, and stay fully conscious so the transmutation Tolle described occurs.

The conclusion of each circle could be a time of reflection. Each person could briefly share how it felt to hold and transmute their pain, if they desired to. In this way, pain-body circles could help individuals to disidentify from the pain-body within, as Tolle promotes. The only way the pain-body can remain intact is when it gets you to identify with it, or when it lives through you,[9] according to Tolle.

Pain-Body Hotline

A free phone hotline open to calls 24-hours a day will mean a person with an active pain-body could call to express their resistance to feeling it.

This would be a Pain-Body Hotline. The person working the hotline will offer support during this time by listening, but mainly holding Presence for the individual in pain. What a relief for the person in the grips of the pain-body!

For it is so much easier to face and transmute your pain-body when someone else is supporting you, and is being the space for you. It wouldn't matter that the two individuals were thousands of miles away. Presence is universal; it is everywhere.

When Brian and I lived across the country from each other, I could actually feel the transmutation process occurring, during pain-body calls with my "pain-body partner." Presence defies the boundaries of space and of time.

Conscious Breathing

Each meeting would start and end with one of Tolle's portals to the present moment: taking a conscious breath. Just a 2-3 minute meditation in which the group would sit in stillness and breath consciously together. Such breathing, especially performed among a group of people, generates the energy of presence.

Starting the meetings off with conscious breathing would help center people who have just come from the busy outside world (or their minds). In the same way, ending the meetings with conscious breathing would encourage people to remain fully present as the leave.

A short 1 or 2 minute conscious breathing meditation could occur in the middle of Community meetings, to keep the group alert and in the Now.

Accessibility

Community of Presence meetings should be available everywhere, not just in a few select cities. People of all ages, socioeconomic statues, cultural backgrounds, ethnicities, and ways of life should have access to the Community.

Moreover, meetings could be held 7 days a week, 365 days a year. Spirituality groups are often held once a week. But, if you have a dramatic argument with your partner on a Wednesday afternoon, you shouldn't have to wait until Saturday to attend a meeting. By then the pain may have taken you over completely, forcing you to engage in self-destructive behaviors. You could be able to attend a Community of Presence meeting that same day to take care of your inner state, and diminish suffering.

We want to bring about the New Earth. Each person's spiritual progress is vital in increasing presence on the planet and transmuting the collective human pain-body.

Imagine if evening meetings were available. Instead of reaching for a beer or watching television to drown out your issues, you could attend a meeting and drop any fictitious problems your mind wants you to believe.

Spiritual Sponsors

Just as there are sponsors in 12 step groups who guide individuals through the challenges of becoming sober, spiritual sponsors would be extremely important in the Community of Presence.

However, in the Community, sponsorship could work differently. Two people who are somehow drawn to each other at a Community meeting would agree to become each other's sponsor. Yes, *both* individuals would be called "sponsor." This is because they would be each other's spiritual partners on the road of awakening.

When Brian helps me out of unconsciousness, this helps him to become more conscious. Although he may not have been faced with a difficulty at the moment, simply talking to me and guiding me through a challenge helps him to return to the present moment as much as it helps me.

Thus, in the Community spiritual sponsors are more like partners. There is no superior or inferior person in the relationship. Like Tolle points out, the teacher and the student become the teaching.

It would be beneficial for each person to have 1 corresponding sponsor. However, it would be fine if an individual did have more than one sponsor.

How to know whom your sponsor should be?

People at Community meetings could simply take time and develop friendships within the group and if there is a connection with a certain person, arrange to be sponsors with that individual. There will be time at the end of each meeting for talking and getting to know one other.

*

Why are spiritual sponsors so important? Such partnerships are so vital because the spiritual journey is not one that *anyone* can walk *alone*. Even the Buddha had such a strong friendship; it is documented that his cousin and friend Ananda walked the journey of enlightenment with him.

Similarly, Jesus had John, "the disciple whom he loved," as well as his other apostles to accompany him during his life on earth. In fact, it is well known that Jesus was upset before his death when he was praying in the garden and his best friends fell asleep. Jesus needed someone by his side to be there with him during the scariest most painful time of his life.

All of us need someone to be there for support, guidance, and true connection. Sponsors would likely become each other's best friends and experience true love. In times of spiritual doubt, heavy pain-body, loss, or any of the other challenges life brings, sponsors could call each other for support and would return to Presence.

Total honesty would be necessary in such relationships. At times, Brian and I would hide our egoic patterns from each other. This is because the ego does not want you to expose it to others, and especially other "spiritual" people. Exposing the mind is weakening it and even dissolving it.

When you express your ego to a trusted friend, this allows both of you to more clearly *see* the ego is not real. When you keep your ego-created thoughts, emotions and behaviors bottled up however, the mind seems truly real and even powerful.

Thus, opening up to your sponsor about your anger or your resistance to being in the present moment, for example, would weaken such mind-created feelings and patterns.

There have been countless times when I've been trapped in my mind, decided to call Brian about it, and after twenty-minutes of conversation, I end up not only feeling so much better and free, but also laughing at the ego within and seeing it as phantom.

*

Eckhart Tolle's illustration of love totally opposes what most of the world considers love to be. He simply, yet beautifully explains that, "to love is to recognize yourself in another."[10]

What this means is the Consciousness in you *sees* the Consciousness in the person you love. In other words, love is not merely appreciating the physical or psychological aspects of your loved one but truly noticing and touching the spacious awareness within their human form.

The divine within the material. When this happens it is the deepest, truest connection two humans can ever have.
If you experience this type of love and while being still inside, really look your loved one in the eye and connect with their Consciousness, you will likely feel overwhelmed and will probably shed a couple tears.

This is because when witnessing the other as pure Consciousness, you witness God: you witness your true self. Compared to that, a clingy, possessive romantic relationship or friendship is practically nothing, and are filled with conflict and dissatisfaction as Tolle explains.

When you witness Consciousness in another human, it simply means that you sense the stillness within them. The silent, empty, space of nothingness. In that nothingness, is everything. It is the dimension of God within the impermanent human form. That is true love. And it is not only accessible in romantic relationships.

Tolle describes how true love can be experienced not only with humans but also with trees, flowers and animals. When present, I have experienced simply looking at an orchid plant, or into my adorable cat Bayo's green eyes and actually *seeing* Consciousness.

During such times I've shed tears of bliss and stayed present long after. For when you are still and look at a flower or into the eyes of an animal or your partner without thought, you reconnect with *your* true essence.

You see God face to face. And seeing, or being one with Consciousness is unlike anything that the physical world could ever offer.

With the following words, Tolle explains most romantic relationships are more like "love/hate relationships":

> You cannot love your partner one moment and attack him or her the next. True love has no opposite. If your love has an opposite, then it is not love but a strong ego-need for a more complete and deeper sense of your self, a need that the other person cannot meet for you. It is the ego's substitute for salvation or God."

The words "strong ego-need for a more complete and deeper sense of your self," point to manipulation in human relationships. And this occurs not just in romantic relationships but also in friendships and among family members and co-workers. Most relationships are sadly there for the ego to strengthen itself and become more.

"If you are my friend I am more complete. Therefore do what I command and be who I want you to be so we can remain friends," is the ego's thought process.

In family relationships love is often only present when needs are met. For instance, if two adult siblings disagree on something, it is common for them to go periods without speaking to one another.

Or, if an adult child drops out of college or goes their own way in life there is often shame, criticism and even avoidance from the parent. We can see such relationships, which are prevalent, are not based on true love.

Because, as Tolle teaches, you cannot love someone and then hate them when something goes wrong, for

true love has no opposite.

Most relationships are in fact ego-based relationships that lack or rarely manifest true love, according to Tolle.

The reason I bring up the lack of true love in human relationships is because within the Community, true love relationships *will* form. How do I know this? The relationship among Brian and I is one of true love. We often connect so deeply we feel our inner-bodies. Although we have been through challenges together at times we snap out of it quickly. We don't hold grudges because we see there's nothing to forgive.

What is more we are supportive to one another at all times, accept whatever each other is experiencing without judgment and have no expectations in our friendship.

Our relationship is platonic and always will be. Fittingly, we are of differing sexual orientations. However, the love between Brian and I is most likely as strong as most married couples. In fact we have called each other "soul mates."

It amazes me how often our lives are so parallel. It's common I call him to express a certain issue only to find he is going through the exact same issue in his life. In fact, our spiritual growth is also aligned. For example, when he had overcome spiritual aloneness, I too had let go of such feelings.

I believe that in the Community, there will be the blossoming of such friendships. And this development of pure love among humans will surely impact the world as a whole. It will bring presence power to the human race. "All you need is love."

Nature Walks

I have learned from Tolle's works and lectures, as well as from personal experience how vital nature is in awakening and staying present on a daily basis. Nature is in fact one of the easiest and most potent of the many openings into presence.

Walk and you can gauge where your mind is at, and how your ego is doing. How long does it take before the prattle of thoughts and concern is replaced by observing nature-the sky, clouds, trees, plants, animal tracks, birds, the breeze- very soon you will be tuned into the universe which surrounds you, rather than the self-made world within.

Each time you walk, you are strengthening your ability to focus on what is before you: the here and now. The relationship you build with the natural universe will come into play in your life in magical, myriad ways. This relationship helps tear down the walls and clutter inside.

When connected to nature you are deeply connected to yourself, or who you really are. More specifically, when you give nature your full attention, Consciousness becomes aware of itself, Tolle describes. This could be simply your pet dog or cat, a small cactus plant in your home or even more effective, being outside, surrounded by air, sky, trees, animals and the ground.

For anyone who is semi-awakened, being in nature provides almost instant access to returning to the present moment.

Have you not walked outside in a while? Do you find yourself more tense, more easily distracted? Sometimes we go without the disciplines we know we should be employing. Come back to them- walk again for the first time in a while, and the relief is more. The serenity and beauty is more obvious, mysterious, alluring. This is the natural universe welcoming you back.

*   *   *

Around the same time I read Tolle, I lived with my sister and her husband with their adorable pet dog Chelsea, a Boxer-Collie mix. One of the best time periods of my life was living there and walking Chelsea each night when it got dark, for an average of two hours. It felt so good to walk in nature with another being- more importantly, a being that didn't engage in thought provoking conversation.

Chelsea never said a word, besides an occasional bark when noticing another dog. She never once complained to me about all of her problems, because she simply doesn't have problems. Because of this we experienced true connection. She glanced up at me and smiled often and was so very present in the moment.

Therefore it was a joyous experience to walk with Chelsea each night. I felt connected to her and she represented Nature. There was no mind there to put on airs, tell stories or manipulate. Further, on our nightly walks I grew more deeply connected to the natural world.

I would look up at the night sky and see and feel the space between me and the stars. I would actually sense that space within myself Tolle has written about. I would pause and look at my surroundings, the people, the flowers, and the animals in stillness.

During that time period, walking with Chelsea at night became one of the biggest and most meaningful spiritual practices I could engage in. And Chelsea was always very patient when I would stop and pause for a moment to look at a tree. Looking at a tree in stillness, I would sense its rootedness in life and feel my own. I bring this example up because reconnecting with nature during that time period was not only healing but promoted my own spiritual growth and boosted presence power within me.

And, I believe nature, and specifically, taking walks in nature could be a very important activity within the Community of Presence.

* * *

It is becoming well-known that spending time in nature, walking barefoot on the ground and being exposed to sunlight provides actual physical benefits and can heal or reduce the effects of certain physical and psychological illnesses. And, the impact of the natural world on one's spiritual growth and level of presence is immense.

The relationship of being in nature and becoming awake is well documented throughout history. Buddha traveled outdoors and lived in caves. It is well known that he sat underneath a Bodhi tree and became enlightened. Henry David Thoreau came to know himself, the nature of humanity and civilization as a whole during his experiences living outside. He stated, "I took a walk in the woods and came out taller than the trees."[12] These words obviously point to an inner expansion of spiritual awareness Thoreau experienced while spending time in the great outdoors.

And of course, there's Eckhart Tolle who lived outside on a park bench post-awakening and experienced bliss. Tolle's love for and appreciation of nature is expressed in his written works and lectures.

Nature is necessary when walking the path towards full awakening. Nature, in fact, is who we are. This is why it is important to put down your phone for a bit each day, and discover yourself within the natural world. And, this is why nature should be a fundamental aspect of the Community.

One meeting each week could take place outdoors. During such a meeting, the entire group could take a 30 to 40 minute walk in silence. Then, the group could sit and share what they experienced while being present in nature. There could be multiple times throughout the walk when the group would stop for a minute to simply observe the surroundings in stillness, while hydrating or stretching. Too often, we go to the park with friends and talk the whole time, or listen to music. But, actively being still inside on a walk with other average spiritual Joes would present an opportunity of deepening awareness.

Thoreau put it like this: "there is a subtle magnetism in Nature, which, if we unconsciously yield to it, will direct us aright."[13] The only part about that quote I would change is substituting "unconsciously yield to it" with "consciously recognize." When we take the time to consciously appreciate nature, this enhances our aliveness. When enough individuals begin to truly witness, spend time in and focus on the natural world around them, we will start to see the New Earth with our own eyes.

Reiki/Yoga

Although I've pointed out simply doing Reiki or yoga rarely causes a permanent shift of Consciousness, I did so to make a point. The point being, it is vital to not only transmute one's pain-body in order to fully become awake, but also to join together in Community to strengthen individual and collective Consciousness. That being said, I do believe that practicing both Reiki and yoga are deeply rewarding in and of themselves and are healing practices for many. Thus I propose the Community offer yoga classes as well as Reiki attunement classes and personal Reiki healing sessions.

Yoga or Reiki masters could volunteer their time to lead such sessions. I propose that these classes be free because energy is free and accessible to all and the Community should not be of charge. However, donations can compensate. Reiki and Yoga are important in getting people to feel their inner body and become more present. Reiki could be practiced for a few minutes during each meeting. This would help individuals to discover and pay attention to blocked pain within the body.

Kim Eng often leads movement sessions at her and Tolle's retreats. And this is for a reason: moving the body while conscious allows you to more fully feel and connect with your inner body and also discover any hidden pain.

Service/Volunteering Opportunities

When aligned with Presence, it is only natural that people would have a desire to help those in need. In the Community, weekly or monthly group volunteering opportunities should be available for those who would like to participate.

Eckhart Tolle explains that when people are in touch with Being they positively impact people wherever they go even if they do not say a word. Thus, if a group of people within the Community went out and simply spent time with those in hospitals, prisons, nursing homes, etc., true healing would take place for all involved. Service projects geared towards helping the environment, those in poverty as well as animals would be excellent opportunities to not only help out on the surface layer but also spread presence power and work towards the New Earth at the same time.

Especially for people who are retired or not working, volunteering their time with other Community members would be fulfilling and enjoyable. The important thing to focus on here is service takes you out of yourself. And anything that takes you out of your limited human sense of self is an opening into Consciousness, who you really are. This is one of the reasons why many people across the world enjoy volunteering.

Retreats

Eckhart Tolle has likened spiritual retreats to "greenhouses." Just as greenhouses strengthen vulnerable plants, spiritual retreats provide a safe space for humans to regenerate, find stillness and reemerge in the world more present and able to face the storms of life.

Some spiritual retreats have been life-changing for me. They were invaluable on the path of awakening. Spending a week or weekend in a "greenhouse" environment of presence gives one a boost in presence power.

Furthermore, retreats provide a time of quiet. You can return to yourself and to what truly matters. The outside world often provides challenges as well as busyness and countless demands. These demands can all too easily sweep one's attention away from presence, and towards a total outer-layer focus.

The Community meetings themselves would serve as mini-greenhouses. A daily hour of calm within the storm. Yet, it would also be important for us average spiritual Joes to attend monthly or bi-yearly spiritual retreats with other Community members. And what would these retreats be about? The Now of course.

There would be pain-body circles, conscious breathing meditations as there will be in the daily Community meetings. However, there would be more time for personal rest and stillness, which is invaluable in our current society. People could spend time in total silence and reconnect with their Being.

Moreover, Community members could more deeply connect with one another while on retreat due to the longer time span. This sort of connection often leads to life-long friendships and would most likely generate sponsor relationships as well.

And- spiritual retreats are fun! There are usually fun activities such as games, and sharing jokes. This would allow for humor and release of tension, doorways to the Now.

*

Spiritual retreats are not always rainbows and butterflies. They often provide instant access into the present moment. Thus, spiritual retreats often bring up painful emotions we are unable to feel when engaged in the busy outside world of work and family.

I remember this during the 2014 Tolle and Eng retreat at the Omega Institute. There were long periods of free time during the 5-day retreat in between Eckhart and Kim's lectures.

And because I went to the retreat alone, did not have my computer or any other electronic gadget, I was forced to simply spend the free time being with myself. And what did I discover during that time of no distractions? Pain.

I felt depressed. I remember wanting for time to speed up so I could attend Tolle's hour long talks and not have to face my pain anymore! One time, I drove to a local gas station even though I had a full tank, just to get away for a little. To get away from my thoughts and my pain.

The retreat was invaluable for it forced me to come into contact with and feel my pain. I was able to hold the pain several times and undergo the transmutation of pain Tolle writes of. Therefore, in the Community, retreats would allow individuals to come into contact with their personal pain-body and face it without distractions.

Spiritual retreats should be inexpensive so that all who wanted could attend. For instance, a weekend spiritual retreat should cost around $100-$150 to cover food and boarding. A week-long retreat should perhaps cost $200-$250.

Additionally, scholarships should be offered for those who do not have extra money to spend on a retreat.

This concludes the possible blueprint of the Community of Presence.

ADDICTION

Tolle has said that the strongest addiction is that of unnecessary thinking. But is there a 12-step group for compulsive thinkers? Are there rehabilitation centers for people who are addicted to the unnecessary thoughts their mind constantly creates?

The answer of course is one big No. And, this is why so many millions of people are unable to fully awaken. Because they can't overcome their addiction to thoughts on their own! What stands in between the individual and enlightenment? The mind of course, and the strong pull to identify with thinking.

In any addiction, exposure and sharing with others is truly the only way out. It forces you to break through the heavy denial you have been living in and provides comfort. Because of the group, you are no longer alone in the addiction. In that lies true liberation.

That freedom arises because the addict no longer believes there is something wrong with them. They see the *common* aspect of the addiction; they realize so many others struggle with the same affliction and thus disidentify from it.

The Community of Presence would allow for people to finally break free of the addiction to the mind because such individuals would come together on a consistent basis to expose and weaken the ego and its addictive nature.

We must come together if we want to be free. We cannot live in the dark anymore and keep our egoic thoughts and emotional pain within us. Thus, we have to express it to others who are becoming awakened. "Whatever is exposed to the light, itself becomes light."[14]

*

How do I know that community can free people from the addiction to thinking? I know because I experienced it first-hand. Recently, Brian moved back to Cleveland, Ohio, where I live. In this, he experienced uncertainty.

A new job, living space, being so far away from his Nebraska friends created a lack of worldly security. At the same time, I experienced the loss of a large part of my surface-layer security. Because of this, Brian and I became closer than ever. We now talked more than once a day. We also had the benefit of physically living in the same city.

Driving to local parks together to sit in silence happened every weekend. But, importantly something else happened. Together on the phone one Friday morning I called Brian in a moment of despair. My mind would not leave me alone. It kept churning out thought after thought. Mostly fearful or depressive thoughts about the future. I was in total resistance-yet again.

Brian too had been experiencing such mind-dominance and resistance. During the phone call, we created a realization. Brian firmly said, "Kat, every time you notice a thought, shut the door on it. Simply drop the thought. You have the ability to do this."

The rest of that day, both Brian and I practiced shutting the door on our thoughts. This is something you can try. Whenever a nagging thought appears, picture a small door in your brain, and see the thought trying to enter the door. But, close the door on the thought. Visually see the door being pushed closed. Then take a moment to pause. In that moment of stillness, *feel* the separation between You and the thought that was trying to enter the "door."

When you close the door on a thought, you begin to see that you are not your thoughts. This is an excellent way to get out of the mind. You step back and see that you actually do have a choice. You have the choice to either follow the thought completely and be dominated by the mind or to step back and see it as simply a thought.

If you see the separation between your Consciousness and the thoughts your mind produces, you have the option to remain in awareness.

That same day, Brian and I, by evening, decided to go to a restaurant. As we ate, we remained aware of the gap of separation between Consciousness and thoughts. We observed people and things around us. We effortlessly felt our inner-bodies the entire time. Life was so beautiful, even though 10 hours earlier, before we spoke on the phone, we were both in suffering and resistance.

In the days and weeks that followed, that separation remained. Both of us lost it at times, and this was painful. But we didn't lose it completely. Each time we felt ourselves being drawn back into thought, we called each other on the phone. Through those phone calls, we returned to awareness. Awareness of the thoughts, rather than being completely mind-possessed.

Importantly, we discovered that the thoughts do not go away. They are still there. And this is okay- it just is. It doesn't mean we failed because our mind continued to churn out thoughts. However, we could now see them as thoughts and choose not to follow them or believe in them.

I mention this because it is a clear representation of the role of Community in breaking the addiction to thinking. I could not have done it on my own. If I didn't call Brian that Friday morning when I was totally lost in thought, the realization would not have occurred.

Neither of us would have reached that point of being able to so clearly see the thoughts and disidentify with them. The mind is so strong in humans that we need one another. Brian and I needed each other. And—we continue to rely on each other for support and for accountability.

Currently, we are still in the stage of being able to see our thoughts and choosing to step back from them. However, we are like sprouts. Just as fragile sprouts need shelter, Brian and I need each other. We are not yet strong flowers. Sprouts need protection from the winds of life. They may be placed in a greenhouse. Brian and I are each other's protection from the winds of mind-possession.

So, we check in on each other and share any difficulties in remaining present during this time.

In the Community of Presence, people could find protection and enhancement of awareness through the support of other awakened individuals. And in this, addiction to thinking, a world-wide affliction, will break down and eventually cease to exist.

WE CAN ANSWER
EACH OTHER'S QUESTIONS

Anyone who has been to an Eckhart Tolle retreat or who has listened to his lectures knows that so many people walking the spiritual journey often live in confusion. At the Tolle retreat I attended, I remember his team announced it was Q&A time.

So many hands instantly shot up. At the core, although they varied in subject matter, the questions nearly all had to do with exactly what this book is about: *how do I become totally free?*

The questions were basically some variation of that. People traveled from across the globe because they became awake inside but wanted desperately to live like Tolle does, free of the mind. Because they live in a state of confusion, half conscious, half stuck in thinking, life for average spiritual Joes can at times be painful. This is why their questions are so important to them.

In the Community of Presence, people can ask questions for free, at local meetings on a daily basis. We can, as a group, provide answers.

For we all have the Truth within us. Individuals would learn as much from such meetings as they would from attending a Tolle retreat. It's time to broaden the horizons of the world's spiritual resources. It's time for us to answer each other's questions and be each other's teachers.

WHAT ABOUT THE FREQUENCY HOLDERS?

For those whom Eckhart Tolle describes as the "frequency holders," living in the world can be quite difficult. What feels natural to many frequency holders is living a simple life. This often does not include higher education or even a career, or at least not a stressful job working 8 hours a day. People who naturally lack a strong drive to create or constantly be doing things do not have it easy.

Why? Because the world constantly bombards everyone with the message when you reach adulthood you must work, or you are nothing. The sad but common message of our society is work, work, work and make a good living.

But for the frequency holders of the world there is usually very little desire or true motivation to go out and "make a living." Such people do not cope well in stressful situations and a typical day of making a living is often filled with stress. Some people just want to live, as the animals, doing simple things in the moment.

Very much like a cat, a person who is a frequency holder may thoroughly enjoy staying at home all day, possibly going for a walk, sitting in nature, watching the birds and people who pass by, observing the sky and flowers, relaxing, drawing, writing, singing, appreciating life, ect.

And of course, going to the grocery store, doing chores, taking care of one's health and seeing friends and family members when needed. But an all around mad rush to make money and even the thought of working in a building for 8-9 hours a day to survive seems almost unbearable to any frequency holder.

However, on the New Earth, frequency holders will have it easier. This is because on the New Earth people will not have to work 40-50 hours a week just to "make it." There will no longer be the insane inequality in payment among people.

In the current world, there is a huge unfair divide in income. Whereas one person may work at a desk each day planning projects and make $40 an hour, another person may be on their feet all day cleaning floors and only make $7 an hour. CEO's of companies may earn $300,000 a year while a restaurant worker who must physically work harder and break their back all day barely takes home $18,000 a year. And if you're a woman just go ahead and deduct 30% off of both of those salaries.

What's more insane is people who act in movies or play on national sports teams make millions of dollars a year when so many others make next to nothing working crucial jobs, such as cleaning hospital rooms. This is truly the insanity of the human ego, which is of course running our planet.

And then you look at countries such as India or Africa where millions live each day without clean water, food, shelter or access to medicine and other resources. Such people live in poverty most individuals of the United States could not even imagine.

However, on the New Earth, insane misallocation of resources will no longer exist. There will be fairness in the dividing of money and other assets. As the ego loses its strength in the world the need to subjugate other human beings will lessen while fairness and equality expand, touching more and more people.

Though it is difficult to imagine it right now, in the New Earth the way humans live will be quite different. We will spend more time with our family and friends. We will spend more time in nature. There will be a great reduction in stress and an immense decrease in stress-related illnesses and afflictions. Moreover, people will not have to "scrape by" to survive, or go without basic necessities while others live in mansions and own 700 pairs of shoes. The fullness of life will not only be a reality within people but also on the outer layer of their lives. Because with so many people will live consciously, few will starve. Income will be more equal, leading to fewer hours at work.

And the sharing of resources is just one example of *thousands* of how the world will be an entirely different, better place to call home.

> Then I saw a new heaven and a new earth, for the old heaven and the old earth had disappeared.[15]

Tolle's *A New Earth* gave us everything we needed to bring about the rising of a new, better world. Now its time to implement all previous efforts, together.

TOO MANY DARK NIGHTS OF THE SOUL

In an interview for a book by John W. Parker, titled *Dialogues With Emerging Spiritual Teachers*, Eckhart Tolle stated:

> Humankind as a whole has been through such vast suffering that one could almost say that every human has suffered enough now. No further suffering is necessary...Spiritual teachings are coming through...many humans will be able to break through without any further need for suffering.[16]

In *The Power of Now*, Tolle explains humans have needed suffering to become awakened, but by living in the Now, suffering becomes unnecessary.

However, the book was published in 1997, nearly 20 years ago, and it seems as though suffering is only *increasing* on the planet, year after year, day after day. Importantly, this is also the case for followers of Tolle's teachings. Indeed, individuals who *recognize* the Truth and importance of living in the present moment **still find themselves creating suffering**.

Moreover, it is all too common for people who are awakening to experience what is well know in spirituality as 'The Dark Night of the Soul.'

The Dark Night is an experience of deep emotional pain that overwhelms a person and sends them plummeting into the depths of their soul. This may be offset by an immense loss such as the death of one's spouse or child, or simply it could be the peak of an ongoing depression.

Then at some point, they wake up and feel better, even lighter. This often leads people to assume they are now finally free. They may think, "wow, maybe I fully made it through and I no longer need any more suffering." However, such individuals continue to suffer and experience Dark Nights of the Soul.

After each 'Dark Night' they hope this time will be the end of pain and will bring full enlightenment.

People who have endured major losses and Dark Nights of the Soul do experience a shift in Consciousness and become more awake after such experiences. However, they often do not become fully free and live as Tolle does with a cessation of suffering.

Total enlightenment, total wakefulness is generally not the case. While still experiencing presence, for the shift of Consciousness is permanent as Tolle points out, such people eventually find themselves stuck in the heavy conditioning of the mind once again and emotional pain ensues.

Yes, people who have experienced extreme loss or break down have woken up, but it's not extremely common they wake up for *good*. Many people who read *The Power of Now* years ago when it first came out still suffer. Lets look at why so many people continue to go suffer while on the spiritual path, and even experience extreme suffering, or Dark Nights of The Soul.

Personally, I have experienced a shift in Consciousness. In fact through heavy suffering in my life I came to read Tolle's teachings and deeply appreciate them.

However, I am an average spiritual Joe. I still get lost in the mind from time to time, experience worry and the emotions of the pain-body. And, since reading Tolle's works, I've endured multiple Dark Nights of the Soul, and still suffer.
Why is this?

Quite simply because the conditioning of the human mind is so strong. This is why myself and other average spiritual Joes continue to suffer even though we know the Truth and are connected to it.

The human ego is very much in tact and on our own we simply cannot fully break through. Moreover, the pain-body that lives within us is still alive, even though we work on transmuting it at times.

This is why the Community of Presence is so necessary right now. Millions have experienced heavy suffering, have come to know the Truth of Tolle's teachings and experience a shift in Consciousness—but still suffer and cause others to suffer. It is therefore apparent that such people must come together to generate enough presence power so that suffering will truly *no longer be necessary* for humans. It's time to come together so that we no longer have to experience the all-familiar Dark Night of the Soul.

* * *

For thousands of years there has been human suffering. For thousands of years there have been spiritual teachers and teachings. Yet, suffering and spiritual teachings obviously have not been enough to wake the majority of people up fully.

We still live in the Old World where most people are sleep-walking. Therefore, we need something new. *The Power of Now* came out almost 2 decades ago. Will we spend another 20 years living our lives as average spiritual Joes, awake but not fully enlightened and still experiencing mind-created misery? Or can we take the next necessary step of the evolution of the world and join as a Community of people devoted to Presence?

*

Brian and I want for there to be a Community of Presence. We want to live in the New Earth. We want for people of all socioeconomic statuses, races, religions, and walks of life, to be able to join together in the process of awakening. Whether you are very busy, have children, are married, or are single and have lots of time on your hands. At this point in time the world needs Community.

It's truly that simple. Because we *want* to live in the present moment. We want to enter the Now through the many portals Tolle and other spiritual teachers beautifully offer us. But the old pain and egoic mind conditioning prevent us from wholeheartedly doing so on our own. We may practice feeling the inner body at one moment but then get lost worrying about the future the next.

Over time an inner-split or inner-struggle becomes glaringly apparent. We live with one foot in and one foot out of the kingdom of heaven. We feel presence within ourselves but then hear our mind spitting out constant complaints and negative thoughts.

How could it be that someone deeply realized the truth of living in the present moment and then leave it behind?

Because they couldn't walk the path on their own. The mind is too strong. That collective mind needs a collective Community to come along and break it down for good, dissolve it forever. Community is our true strength, our power. Let us form the Community and build the New Earth.

To every average spiritual Joe- we are calling you. Help build the Community of Presence. For *any person* who responds to the call of this book, please join us in truly building a better world and a better human existence for all people. Start a Community of Presence meeting in the city where you live. See that the world is ready for the New Earth to arise. Let's come together to build a global Community towards total awakened living.

NOTES

Introduction

1. Tolle, Eckhart. *A New Earth: Awakening to Your Life's Purpose*. New York, N.Y: Dutton/Penguin Group, 2005. Print.

2. Tolle, Eckhart. *The Power of Now: A Guide to Spiritual Enlightenment*. Vancouver, B.C: Namaste Pub, 2004. Print.

3. Tolle, Eckhart. *The Power of Now: A Guide to Spiritual Enlightenment*. Vancouver, B.C: Namaste Pub, 2004. Print.

4. Tolle, Eckhart. *The Power of Now: A Guide to Spiritual Enlightenment*. Vancouver, B.C: Namaste Pub, 2004. Print.

Chapter 1

1. Matthew 21:12-13 (English Standard Version)

2. Tolle, Eckhart. *A New Earth: Awakening to Your Life's Purpose*. New York, N.Y: Dutton/Penguin Group, 2005. Print.

3. Plato. Rouse, W.H.D., ed. *The Republic Book VII*. Penguin Group Inc. pp. 365–401

Chapter 2

1. Tolle, Eckhart. *A New Earth: Awakening to Your Life's Purpose*. New York, N.Y: Dutton/Penguin Group, 2005. Print. 79

2. Tolle, Eckhart. *The Power of Now: A Guide to Spiritual Enlightenment*. Vancouver, B.C: Namaste Pub, 2004. Print.

3. Tolle, Eckhart. *A New Earth: Awakening to Your Life's Purpose*. New York, N.Y: Dutton/Penguin Group, 2005. Print. 217-218

4. Tolle, Eckhart. *The Power of Now: A Guide to Spiritual Enlightenment*. Vancouver, B.C: Namaste Pub, 2004. Print.

5. Tolle, Eckhart. Lecture

6. Matthew 18:3 (New International Version)

7. Tolle, Eckhart. *The Power of Now: A Guide to Spiritual Enlightenment*. Vancouver, B.C: Namaste Pub, 2004. Print.

8. Tolle, Eckhart. *A New Earth: Awakening to Your Life's Purpose*. New York, N.Y: Dutton/Penguin Group, 2005. Print. 260

9. Tolle, Eckhart. *A New Earth: Awakening to Your Life's Purpose*. New York, N.Y: Dutton/Penguin Group, 2005. Print.

9. Tolle, Eckhart. *The Power of Now: A Guide to Spiritual Enlightenment*. Vancouver, B.C: Namaste Pub, 2004. Print.

10. Tolle, Eckhart. *A New Earth: Awakening to Your Life's Purpose*. New York, N.Y: Dutton/Penguin Group, 2005. Print.

11. Tolle, Eckhart. *A New Earth: Awakening to Your Life's Purpose*. New York, N.Y: Dutton/Penguin Group, 2005. Print. 183-184

12. Wilson, T. D., D. A. Reinhard, E. C. Westgate, D. T. Gilbert, N. Ellerbeck, C. Hahn, C. L. Brown, and A. Shaked. "Just Think: The Challenges of the Disengaged Mind." *Science* 345.6192 (2014): 75-77. Web.

13. Tolle, Eckhart. *A New Earth: Awakening to Your Life's Purpose*. New York, N.Y: Dutton/Penguin Group, 2005. Print.

14. Tolle, Eckhart. *The Power of Now: A Guide to Spiritual Enlightenment*. Vancouver, B.C: Namaste Pub, 2004. Print.

15. Tolle, Eckhart. *A New Earth: Awakening to Your Life's Purpose*. New York, N.Y: Dutton/Penguin Group, 2005. Print. Chapter 4

16. Tolle, Eckhart. *A New Earth: Awakening to Your Life's Purpose*. New York, N.Y: Dutton/Penguin Group, 2005. Print.

17. Tolle, Eckhart. *A New Earth: Awakening to Your Life's Purpose*. New York, N.Y: Dutton/Penguin Group, 2005. Print.

18. Tolle, Eckhart. *A New Earth: Awakening to Your Life's Purpose*. New York, N.Y: Dutton/Penguin Group, 2005. Print. 148

19. Tolle, Eckhart. *The Power of Now: A Guide to Spiritual Enlightenment*. Vancouver, B.C: Namaste Pub, 2004. Print. 38

20. Tolle, Eckhart. *The Power of Now: A Guide to Spiritual Enlightenment*. Vancouver, B.C: Namaste Pub, 2004. Print. 192

21. Frost, Robert. *North of Boston.* New York: Henry Holt and Company, 1915; Bartleby.com, 1999. www.bartleby.com/118/.

22. Tolle, Eckhart. *The Power of Now: A Guide to Spiritual Enlightenment*. Vancouver, B.C: Namaste Pub, 2004. Print.

Chapter 3

1. Hafiz, *The Gift*. New York: Penguin, Arkana, 1999. Translated by Daniel Ladinsky

2. John 15:5 (New International Version); Tolle, Eckhart. *A New Earth: Awakening to Your Life's Purpose*. New York, N.Y: Dutton/Penguin Group, 2005. Print.

3. Tolle, Eckhart. *Stillness Speaks*. Vancouver: Namaste Pub., 2003. Print.

4. Psalm 46:10 (New International Version)

5. Verrecchio, Louie. "Lord, I Am Not Worthy." *Catholic Exchange*. 23 July 2010. Web. 07 Apr. 2016.

6. Tolle, Eckhart. *The Power of Now: A Guide to Spiritual Enlightenment*. Vancouver, B.C: Namaste Pub, 2004. Print. 11-12

7. Tolle, Eckhart. *The Power of Now: A Guide to Spiritual Enlightenment*. Vancouver, B.C: Namaste Pub, 2004. Print. 4

8. Matthew 4:1-4 (New International Version)

9. Matthew 17 (New International Version)

10. Katie, Byron, and Stephen Mitchell. *Loving What Is: Four Questions That Can Change Your Life*. New York: Harmony, 2002. Print.

11. Tolle, Eckhart. *Eckhart Tolle's Findhorn Retreat: Stillness amidst the World*. Novato, CA: New World Library, 2006. Print.

12. Tolle, Eckhart. *The Power of Now: A Guide to Spiritual Enlightenment*. Vancouver, B.C: Namaste Pub, 2004. Print.

13. Tolle, Eckhart. *A New Earth: Awakening to Your Life's Purpose*. New York, N.Y: Dutton/Penguin Group, 2005. Print.

14. Tolle, Eckhart. *The Power of Now: A Guide to Spiritual Enlightenment*. Vancouver, B.C: Namaste Pub, 2004. Print. 38

15. Tolle, Eckhart. *The Power of Now: A Guide to Spiritual Enlightenment*. Vancouver, B.C: Namaste Pub, 2004. Print.

16. Tolle, Eckhart. *A New Earth: Awakening to Your Life's Purpose*. New York, N.Y: Dutton/Penguin Group, 2005. Print.

Chapter 4

1. Tolle, Eckhart. *A New Earth: Awakening to Your Life's Purpose*. New York, N.Y: Dutton/Penguin Group, 2005. Print. 258

2. Tolle, Eckhart. *A New Earth: Awakening to Your Life's Purpose*. New York, N.Y: Dutton/Penguin Group, 2005. Print.

3. Tolle, Eckhart. *The Power of Now: A Guide to Spiritual Enlightenment*. Vancouver, B.C: Namaste Pub, 2004. Print. 64

4. Osho. *Freedom: The Courage to Be Yourself*. New York: St. Martin's Griffin, 2004. Print. 133-134

5. Einstein, Albert, Helen Dukas, and Banesh Hoffmann. *Albert Einstein, the Human Side: New Glimpses from His Archives*. Princeton, NJ: Princeton UP, 1979. Print.

6. Tolle, Eckhart. *The Power of Now: A Guide to Spiritual Enlightenment*. Vancouver, B.C: Namaste Pub, 2004. Print.

7. Tolle, Eckhart. *A New Earth: Awakening to Your Life's Purpose*. New York, N.Y: Dutton/Penguin Group, 2005. Print. 184

8. Tolle, Eckhart. *A New Earth: Awakening to Your Life's Purpose*. New York, N.Y: Dutton/Penguin Group, 2005. Print.

9. Caltabiano, Anna. "Loneliness in the Age of Social Networking." *The Huffington Post*. TheHuffingtonPost.com, 1 July 2014. Web. 08 Jan. 2016.

10. Tolle, Eckhart. *A New Earth: Awakening to Your Life's Purpose*. New York, N.Y: Dutton/Penguin Group, 2005. Print.

11. Tolle, Eckhart. *A New Earth: Awakening to Your Life's Purpose*. New York, N.Y: Dutton/Penguin Group, 2005. Print. 293 .

12. "Eckhart Tolle: Oprah Webcast (Chapter 1) Transcription Excerpt." *Eckhart Tolle: Oprah Webcast (Chapter 1) Transcription Excerpt*. Web. 07 Nov. 2015.

13. "Adult Obesity Facts." *Centers for Disease Control and Prevention*. Centers for Disease Control and Prevention, 21 Sept. 2015. Web. 01 Aug. 2015.

14. Gunnars, Kris. "How Sugar Hijacks Your Brain and Makes You Addicted." *Authority Nutrition*. Authority Nutrition, 26 Jan. 2013. Web. 09 Sept. 2015.

15. Often attributed to Albert Einstein; Source unknown.

Chapter 5

1. Tolle, Eckhart. *A New Earth: Awakening to Your Life's Purpose*. New York, N.Y: Dutton/Penguin Group, 2005. Print.

2. "Marcus Aurelius." BrainyQuote.com. Xplore Inc, 2016. 08 October 2015.
http://www.brainyquote.com/quotes/quotes/m/marcusaure108217.html

3. "Albert Einstein." BrainyQuote.com. Xplore Inc, 2016. 14 November 2015.
http://www.brainyquote.com/quotes/quotes/a/alberteins129798.html

4. John 15:19 (New International Version)

5. Matthew 18:19-20 (New King James Version)

6. Tolle, Eckhart. *The Power of Now: A Guide to Spiritual Enlightenment*. Vancouver, B.C: Namaste Pub, 2004. Print. 42

7. John 5:30 (King James Bible)

8. Matthew 7:13-14 (New International Version)

9. Tolle, Eckhart. *The Power of Now: A Guide to Spiritual Enlightenment*. Vancouver, B.C: Namaste Pub, 2004. Print. 37

10. Tolle, Eckhart. *A New Earth: Awakening to Your Life's Purpose*. New York, N.Y: Dutton/Penguin Group, 2005. Print. 105

11. Tolle, Eckhart. *The Power of Now: A Guide to Spiritual Enlightenment*. Vancouver, B.C: Namaste Pub, 2004. Print. 151

12. Lane, Brad. "Inspirational Quotes to Get You Wanting to Explore Nature." *Pacsafe Blog*. Pacsafe, 28 Jan. 2014. Web. 17 Nov. 2016.

13. Thoreau, Henry David. *Excursions, Poems and Familiar Letters V2*. Whitefish: Kessinger, LLC, 2007. Print.

14. Ephesians 5:13

15. Revelation 21:1 (New Living Translation)

16. Parker, John W. *Dialogues with Emerging Spiritual Teachers*. Fort Collins, CO: Sagewood, 2001. Print.

Kat Van Gunten is a caregiver and writer who lives in Cleveland Heights, Ohio. Alongside her spiritual sponsor, Brian Kratko, she is passionate about bringing people together to celebrate the present moment. You may reach her to brainstorm about the New Earth and how to create a Community of Consciousness around you at katvangunten@gmail.com.

Least Bittern Books is a small press out of Henry County, KY which specializes in poetry and art. This is the first Spirituality book on the imprint. Past titles include:

Come Here by Victor Clevenger (2016)
Coyote Highway by Charles Potts (2016)
Under the Mountain Born by John Swain (2015)
earth notes and other poems by e b bortz (2015)
Look Up and Up by Bree (2015)
Poets in the Pond Anthology (2015)
Pilgrim & Martel by Charles Potts (2016)

Constantly seeking strong, singular voices. Send queries to leastbitternbooks@gmail.com